Teach Me About God
Hands-On Bible Lessons
For Active Preschoolers

Michelle Caskey

Inquisitive Minds Press®
Caledonia, MI

Teach Me About God: Hands-On Bible Lessons for Active Preschoolers

© 2008, 2013 Michelle L. Caskey. All rights reserved

Published by *Inquisitive Minds Press*®
Caledonia, MI 49316
www.InquisitiveMindsPress.com

Printed in the United States of America

ISBN-10: 0988544423
ISBN-13: 978-0-9885444-2-0

Cover and Companion Download Illustrations by Melanie Rankin

Interior page layout by Michelle L. Caskey

This book is dedicated to my sons, Ben and Sam. God gave me such an amazing blessing when He allowed me to homeschool you boys. I cherish all of the time and the learning we've been able to do together. You are both growing up to be godly young men and your dad and I thank God for that. I love you both!

Who God Is
God Exists – You can be sure God is real and powerful

Lesson One – God's Big Power

Materials: Tape measure
Empty Tin Cans or Empty Paper Towel Rolls
Five Small, Soft Foam Balls or Balls Made of
     Crumbled Paper

Preparation: None

Story:

    At the time of our story, there were some enemies who wanted to take over God's land. One day, the evil men wanted to fight God's people. This time, they brought a super tall man named Goliath. He was over 9 feet tall. (Show child how tall this is using the tape measure.)

    Goliath did not love God. He was proud and loved himself more than other people. He would brag every day and ask for someone to come and fight him.

    Around that same time, there was a young boy named David who helped to take care of his dad's sheep. David loved God. He knew God helped him to take care of the sheep. As a shepherd, David had to protect the sheep from lions and bears. David relied on God to help him with this hard job. David had many brothers who were soldiers. They were off protecting God's people from the evil men who were trying to take over God's land.

    One day, David came to bring food to his brothers who were fighting. While he was there, Goliath came out and shouted at God's army. David could not believe his ears! He knew that God was bigger than any man, especially someone who was mean to God's people.

    David knew that God would win the battle. David talked to King Saul about fighting Goliath. David shared with Saul how God had helped him fight a lion and a bear to protect the sheep.

    Saul saw David's strong faith in God and he decided to let David try to fight Goliath. Saul gave David his heavy armor to wear. When David tried it on, it was too big.

    Instead, David found five round stones from a creek and put them in his pocket. (Show your child the five foam balls) Then Goliath came. He looked at young David and he laughed. Goliath told David he would feed him to the birds.

    David said, "You may come with your armor and spears, but I come to you in the name of the Lord. Today the Lord will give you to me. I will kill you. Everyone here will know that God did this. The battle belongs to God. God will win!"

    David quickly ran to meet Goliath. He put a stone in his sling and hit Goliath right between the eyes. Goliath fell back and died. With God's help, David did it! God sure is powerful! Hooray!

Lesson:
1. Read the story to your child.
2. Discuss with your child that God helped David to have good aim and to be able to hit Goliath with his slingshot. Talk about how God also wants to help us just like He helped David.
3. Ask your child if he thinks he has good aim.
4. Set up the cans or cardboard rolls on the edge of a table.
5. Have your child stand back far enough from the table that they have to aim to be able to knock them down.
6. Have your child throw the balls to try to knock down the objects.

Lesson Two – David's Bag of Stones

Materials: NIrV Bible – 1 Samuel 17:1-50
5 Flat Rocks and 1 Larger Rock
Various Colors of Paint
Permanent Black Marker
Masking Tape

Preparation:
1. (optional) You may want to go outside with your child and search for the rocks.
2. Using the masking tape, mark off a square approximately 12" x 12" on the ground – you may want to do this outside on concrete to prevent scratching your floor.

Lesson:
1. Read the story of David and Goliath out of the Bible.
2. Let your child paint the rocks however they would like.
3. Using the marker, help your child to write the letters D-A-V-I-D – one letter on each of the smaller rocks.
4. Help them to write a G on the larger rock.
5. Tell your child to place the G rock in the center of the square.
6. Have your child sit at the edge of the square and try sliding their rocks to try to knock Goliath outside of the square.
7. Remind your child that God is very powerful and He wants to help us just like He helped David.

Lesson Three – Fire on the Mountain

Materials: Gray, Red, Orange and Yellow Construction Paper
                Scissors
                Glue
                Crayons or Markers

Preparation: None

Story:

Elijah was a man who loved God. King Ahab was a bad king who did not love and obey God. In fact, Ahab worshipped a fake god. One day, God told Elijah to pray that it wouldn't rain. God wanted to punish King Ahab for being naughty. Sure enough, it stopped raining all over the land. Elijah had someone tell King Ahab why it had stopped raining. The reason was that God was very sad because Ahab worshipped a fake god instead of the One True God.

King Ahab was angry. He told everyone in the land to look for Elijah so that he could kill him. God took care of Elijah, though, and kept King Ahab from finding and hurting him.

Elijah prayed that it wouldn't rain for three years. And God didn't send rain for three years. That is a very long time. Everything in the land was dry and dying.

Finally, God told Elijah to go see King Ahab. Elijah challenged the king to a contest. He told the king to bring the people who worshipped a fake god instead of the real God. These people would build an altar to their God. Then they would pray to their fake god and ask him to send fire to come down and burn up the wood on the altar. Elijah would also build an altar – but his altar would be for the real God. Elijah would pray to the real God and ask Him to send fire to come down and burn up the wood on His altar.

The king's men prayed and prayed to their fake god but no fire came. Elijah smiled. He knew that a fake god could do nothing to help the people.

Elijah poured a bunch of water on his altar. Then he prayed to the real God and asked Him to send fire. Instantly, God brought fire down from heaven which burned up the wood and the water!

When the people saw this, they fell down to the ground and cried, "The Lord is God! The Lord is God!"

Elijah then told King Ahab to go because a heavy rain was coming.

Elijah prayed seven times. Soon a tiny, dark cloud was in the sky. It came closer and closer and then it started to rain. God had again answered Elijah's prayers. The people saw that God was real.

God showed the people that He was real and could do amazing things. The people started to worship Him and love Him.

Lesson:
1. Read the story to your child.
2. Talk to your child about how God is powerful and is the one and only God. Anyone else that people worship is a fake god with no power.
3. Help your child to cut the gray construction paper into rock shapes.
4. Help your child glue the "rocks" to a full piece of paper in the shape of an altar.
5. Help your child to tear strips of red, orange, and yellow paper to be fire flames.
6. Have your child glue the "flames" to the top of the altar.
7. Write "God is No. 1" at the bottom of your child's paper.
8. Let them draw Elijah and decorate their pictures with the crayons or markers.

Lesson Four – Can You Set It On Fire?

Materials: NIrV Bible – 1 Kings 18:15-39
                  Candle
                  Match

Preparation: None

Lesson:
1. Read the story of Elijah and the Prophets of Baal to your child.
2. Light the candle to show them how easily you are able to do it.
3. Pour water on the candle.
4. Now try to light the candle. You won't be able to do it.
5. Explain to your child that is just like in the story – only God was able to light the fire even though it was soaking wet, proving His power.

Lesson Five - The Chariot of Fire

Materials: Photo Albums of Older Family Members
                  Picture of a Chariot (see companion download)

Preparation:
1. Print the chariot from the companion download.
2. Think of something you've learned from someone who is older than you.

Story:

Elijah was God's special messenger. One day, God told Elijah a special secret. God told him that he was going to go to heaven that day. God told Elijah that he would go to heaven in a way that was different from most people.

Elijah's friend, Elisha, was sad. He loved his friend like he was his father. Elijah was older than Elisha and he had taught him many things. Elisha did not want his friend to leave; but, he knew that heaven was a wonderful place and that God would take good care of his friend. He knew that he could trust God.

Suddenly, as they were walking and talking, they heard a loud roaring sound. They saw a chariot of fire and horses of fire. (Show your child the picture of the chariot from the companion download.) It separated the two friends and God took Elijah straight up to heaven in a whirlwind. Elisha saw everything. He was so sad. He tore his clothes, which was a way to show that he was sad and emotional about what had happened. He knew he would never see his friend again.

Elisha looked down and saw Elijah's coat. He knew it was his special coat. It was Elisha's turn to give God's messages to the people. When the people saw Elisha, they knew he had become God's new special messenger.

God is amazing and powerful. He can do anything He wants to do – even take people to heaven in new and different ways.

Lesson:
1. Read the story with your child.
2. Discuss the story with your child. Tell them that God is so powerful that He was able to take Elijah up to heaven in a whirlwind.
3. Look at the photos of your older family members.
4. Share what you've learned from someone older than you.
5. Ask your child if they can think of anything they've learned from someone who is older than them.

Lesson Six – Jesus Walks on Water

Materials: Sprinkling Can, Spray Bottle or Sprinkler

Preparation: None

Story:

Jesus and the disciples were tired. They had just spent lots of time teaching thousands of people and feeding them. Jesus knew that they needed some time to rest – so he told the people to go home. He had his disciples get into a boat and go across to the other side of the lake. Jesus went up on a mountain by himself to pray.

When the boat was far from land, a storm came and rocked the boat. The wind was strong and the waves were high. Late at night, Jesus came out to meet the boat. He was walking on the water. The disciples were terrified when they saw him walking on the lake. "It's a ghost!" they cried out.

Jesus saw that they were afraid and He said to them, "It's me. Don't be afraid."

Peter, one of the disciples, said to Jesus, "Lord, if it's really you, tell me to come to you on the water."

"Come," Jesus said.

So Peter got out of the boat and started walking on the water toward Jesus. Peter was fine as long as he kept his eyes on Jesus. But when he looked away, he noticed the wind blowing hard and he became afraid. Peter began to sink and he said, "Lord, save me!"

Jesus reached down and pulled Peter back up from the water. "Why didn't you believe me?" He said.

Jesus and Peter climbed into the boat and the wind died down. Then the men who were in the boat worshipped Jesus and said, "Truly you are the Son of God."

Lesson:
1. Read the story with your child.
2. Discuss with your child that Jesus is the only one who could walk on water – or help someone else to walk on water. But you can certainly play in water.
3. Play your favorite water games with your child. Use the sprinkling can, spray bottle or sprinkler outside.
4. If it's too cold to play in the water outside, gather all your favorite bathtub toys and let your child play in the bathtub.

Lesson Seven – Hark, Who Goes There?!?

Materials: NIrV Bible – Matthew 14:22-33
      Wax-Type Paper Cup
      Plastic Wrap
      Rubber Band
      Bowl of Water Filled with Objects to look at

Preparation: Cut the bottom out of the cup.

Lesson:
1. Read the story of Jesus Walking on the Water with your child.
2. Ask your child if they have ever seen anyone walk on the water. Talk about how a miracle is something that only God can do. Jesus was certainly powerful if He was able to walk on water, wasn't He?!?
3. Help your child to make a water scope by placing plastic wrap over the bottom opening of the cup and securing it in place with the rubber band.
4. Let your child use their water scope to look at the different objects in the bowl.

Lesson Eight – The Sun Stands Still

Materials: Yellow Construction Paper
              Wide Black Marker
              Scissors
              Glue
              Crayons or Markers
              Yellow, Orange or Gold Yarn or Tinsel (optional)

Preparation: Using the wide marker, draw a large circle and eight or ten triangles on the construction paper.

Story:

When Joshua was the leader of God's people, God did many amazing things. Joshua loved God and tried to always obey Him. Because of this, God blessed Joshua and helped him to win many battles.

God helped Joshua to destroy a city called Ai. This scared the people who lived in Gibeon, which was close to Ai. The people of Gibeon talked with Joshua and made a promise that they would be friends and wouldn't fight each other.

When the other kings in the area heard that they were friends, they got angry. They decided they would attack Gibeon.

The people of Gibeon called out to Joshua, "Help us! We are being attacked!"

God told Joshua not to be afraid – He would cause His people to win the battle. So Joshua marched God's army to Gibeon to help protect their friends.

They marched all night long and took their enemies by surprise. God caused their enemies to be mixed-up and confused. God's army was winning the battle! The enemies started to run away. As they ran, God sent large hailstones from the sky which killed many of the enemies.

Joshua knew they were winning, but they needed more time to totally defeat their enemies. So he prayed and asked God to stop the sun from moving.

God answered Joshua's prayer. The sun stopped moving until God's army had completely defeated their enemies. It stayed still in the sky for about one more full day. Can you imagine one day which was really two days long?!?

God can do anything. He is so powerful! He controls the sun and everything else here on our planet. What an amazing God!

Lesson:
1. Read the story with your child.
2. Discuss with your child how amazing it was that God would stop the sun from moving for a full day. Talk about what a powerful and loving God we have that He would do something that big for His people.
3. Help your child to cut out the circle and the triangles.
4. Have your child make a sun by gluing the triangles to the outside of the circle.
5. Let your child decorate their sun with the crayons, yarn and tinsel.

Who God Is
God and Jesus Love You

Lesson Nine – I'm Lost

Materials: Cotton Balls
                Construction Paper
                Sheep (see companion download)
                Glue
                Scissors

Preparation: Print the sheep from the companion download.

Story:

       Jesus used to go around telling people stories called parables so that they would be able to understand how much God loves us. One day, He told the people this story:

       "Imagine that you are the owner of 100 sheep. One night, as you count them, you find that one sheep is missing. What will you do? Are you going to settle for the 99 other sheep or will you look for the one lost sheep? Of course you will go look for the one lost sheep!"

       "You look in every bush and by every rock. You listen to see if you heard the sound of the sheep. Finally, you find the sheep! When you get back home, you tell everyone the good news and have a party to celebrate."

       Jesus said that God feels that same way about people. Everyone in Heaven is happy when one person starts to believe in God.

       God loves us so much. He will always care for us and make sure that we are safe and protected.

Lesson:
1. Read the story to your child.
2. Discuss with your child how much God loves us that He will come looking for us when we aren't where we should be – which means we are going our own way and not following Him.
3. Help your child to cut out the sheep.
4. Let your child glue the cotton balls onto the sheep.
5. Save this sheep in a safe place for tomorrow's lesson.

Lesson Ten – The Lost Sheep

Materials: NIrV Bible – Luke 15:3-7
                    Sheep you made during yesterday's lesson

Preparation: None

Lesson:
1. Read the story of the lost sheep to your child.
2. Hide the sheep you made during yesterday's lesson around the room.
3. Let your child look for the sheep.

Lesson Eleven – The Prodigal Son

Materials: Books or Magazines (that depict how animals & people live)

Preparation: None

Story:

     Jesus told this story to tell us how much God loves us:

     There once was a man who had two sons. The younger son said to his father, "Father, give me my share of your money." So the father divided his property between his two sons.

     The younger son took the money and everything he had and he went far, far away. He wasted his money doing naughty things and making bad choices. After he had spent everything, there was a severe famine and he began to be in need. So the son took a job feeding pigs. The son was so hungry and he wished he could eat the food he was feeding to the pigs!

     At some point, the son had a good idea. He realized that his father's servants had more food than he did, while he was starving to death. He decided to go back to his father and beg for mercy. He planned to say, "Father, I have treated you badly. I know that I can no longer be your son; but, could you please hire me to be your servant?" With this thought in mind, the boy headed back to his father.

     But while he was a long way off, his father saw him and felt so sorry for him. He ran to his son, threw his arms around him and hugged him.

     The son said, "Father, I have treated you badly. I know that I can no longer be your son; but, could you please hire me to be your servant?"

     The father said to his servants, "Quick! Bring my best robe and put it on him. Put a ring on his finger and sandals on his feet. Let's have a feast and celebrate. For this son of mine was lost but now he is found." So they all began to celebrate.

Lesson:
1. Read the story to your child.
2. Discuss how the prodigal son wanted to do things his way instead of his father's way – and that doesn't make God happy. Talk about how no matter what we've done, God still welcomes us with open arms when we come back to Him.
3. Look through the books or magazines with your child.
4. Have your child observe how the animals live: what they eat, what they do all day, where they sleep, etc.
5. Then have your child observe how people live.
6. Ask your child if they would rather live like an animal or a person.
7. Explain to your child that it was even worse for the prodigal son because he was living with pigs – and pigs are considered unclean by Jewish people – so it was a big insult for him to be eating with the pigs.

Lesson Twelve – Let the Little Children Come to Me

Materials: Small, Wrapped Gift for your child (from dollar store)

Preparation: None

Story:

Jesus was very busy while He was here on earth. He traveled all around healing people and teaching them about God. His disciples traveled around with Jesus and tried to help Him however they could.

In one town, people started bringing their children to Jesus and asking Him to touch them. The disciples told them to take their children away – that Jesus was too busy with more important matters than to have to deal with a bunch of kids.

Jesus heard the disciples and He was upset with them. He said, "Let the little children come to me. Don't try to stop them! I love these children. And everyone needs to believe in Me like a child to get into Heaven."

Then Jesus took the children into His arms. He hugged them and put His hands on them and blessed them.

Lesson:
1. Read the story to your child.
2. Tell your child that you wanted to give them a gift just because you love them. Show them the gift.
3. Explain that as much as you love them, God loves them even more.
4. Hand your child their gift and let them open it

Lesson Thirteen – Jesus Heals a Man with Leprosy

Materials: Baby Powder, Powder Foundation, or other Cosmetics
               Wash Cloth or Wet Wipes

Preparation: Add some water to the baby powder to make a thick paste

Story:

One day, a man with leprosy came up to Jesus and begged Him on his knees, "If you are willing, you can make me clean." People who had leprosy were very sick. They had to stay away from other people. They lived outside of the village and would yell "unclean" whenever someone came by so that people wouldn't get too close to them. And people with leprosy never, ever could touch anyone else for fear they would get them sick.

When Jesus saw this man, He felt sorry for him. Jesus reached out and touched the man. Jesus said, "I am willing to heal you. Be clean!"

The man with the leprosy was instantly healed. Jesus told him not to tell anyone he had been healed, but the man didn't listen. He was so happy that he went about telling everyone he saw that Jesus had healed him.

Lesson:
1. Read the story to your child.
2. Apply the paste to your child's face and arms. Let them do the same to you. Tell your child to imagine what it would feel like if this paste were sores all over their body.
3. Discuss with your child how lonely this man with leprosy must have been. Talk about how Jesus was probably the first person who had touched the man with leprosy in years and years.
4. Ask your child if Jesus could have healed the man without touching him. (yes) Then why did He touch him? (To show the man how much He loved him.)
5. Wash off the paste with the wash cloth.

Lesson Fourteen – Elijah and the Ravens

Materials: Paper Plate
              Raven Body Parts (see companion download)
              Picture of a Raven (see companion download)
              Glue
              Scissors
              Crayons

Preparation:
1. Print the raven body and parts from the companion download.
2. Depending on the skill level of your child, you may want to cut out the raven body parts for your child. If they are capable, you can let them do this as part of their lesson.

Story:

      Elijah was a prophet of God. Elijah would listen to God and would give people messages from God.

      At one time, God told Elijah to give a message to King Ahab. King Ahab was being very naughty worshipping other fake gods. So God decided He would have to punish King Ahab to let him know that he needed to stop.

      Elijah went to King Ahab and gave him this message from God. "King Ahab, God has decided that it isn't going to rain for the next few years. There won't even be any dew on the ground."

      Wow! No rain for a few years?!? God knew that it would be very hard for people to grow food without rain. He was trying to get their attention.

      Elijah also would have had trouble finding food. But God told him to go to a special place east of the Jordan River. He said that Elijah would be able to drink water from a brook. And God sent ravens to bring food to Elijah. (Show your child the picture of the raven from the companion download.)

      Elijah obeyed God. The ravens brought Elijah bread and meat in the morning and bread and meat in the evening. In this way, God took care of Elijah during the drought.

Lesson:
1. Read the story to your child.
2. Discuss with your child how much God loves people. He loved King Ahab enough to punish him to try to get him to see how naughty he was being. He loved Elijah enough to take care of him during the drought.
3. Have your child make a raven by gluing the body parts to the paper plate.
4. Let your child color their raven.

Lesson Fifteen – Jesus Heals a Woman

Materials: Paper Bag

Items with Different Textures (i.e., Cotton Ball, Orange, Golf Ball, Balloon, Sponge, Candle, etc.)

Preparation: Put the items into the bag.

Story:

      There once was a woman who was very sick. She had been bleeding for twelve years! Many doctors had tried to heal her; but, she just kept getting worse and worse.

      When this woman heard about Jesus and that He was nearby, she went to find him. She saw him with a large crowd of people. The woman worked her way through the crowd and got right up behind Jesus. She thought, "If I just touch his clothes, I will be healed." The woman reached out and touched his coat. Immediately, her bleeding stopped and she could tell that her sickness was gone.

      Jesus could feel that He had healed someone. He turned around and said, "Who touched my clothes?"

      The disciples said, "There is a huge crowd of people around you. There are many people touching you."

      But Jesus kept looking around to find the right person. The woman, knowing He was talking about her, fell at Jesus' feet. She was afraid that He would be mad at her. She told Jesus the whole truth.

      Jesus said, "Daughter, your faith has healed you. Go and be healthy."

Lesson:
1. Read the story to your child.
2. Discuss with your child that Jesus already knew who had touched His robe. He just wanted to talk to the woman. He wanted her to realize that He knew about her and that He cared about her.
3. Talk about how we should always talk to Jesus about our needs. When we are lonely or scared or sick, we can ask Him to help us. He really does care about us and wants to help us.
4. Have your child reach into the touch bag. Ask them to try to identify each item by touch before they remove it from the bag.

Lesson Sixteen – Animal Faces

Materials: Paper Plate

                 Crayons
                 Glue
                 Yarn
                 Cotton Balls
                 Construction Paper
                 Picture of Noah's Ark (see companion
                     download)
                 Crayons
Preparation: None

Story:

      God loved all the people He had created. But most of the people began to love things and people more than they loved God. God was sad when He saw how naughty the people were acting. But God also noticed a good man named Noah. Noah still loved and obeyed God. So God decided to use Noah for a big project.

      God told Noah to build a huge boat called an ark. (Show your child the picture of the ark from the companion download.) Noah and his three sons gathered lots of wood and started building the ark.

      The ark took years and years to build. When it was finally done, God sent two of every kind of unclean animal on earth to the ark. God sent seven pairs of every kind of clean animal on earth to the ark.

      Then God told Noah to go into the ark and to take his whole family with him. Once they were safely on the ark, God shut the door. Noah and his family waited to see what would happen.

      Then the rain began to fall. God sent rain for 40 days and 40 nights. That's longer than a month! The water covered the whole earth and the only things that were alive on earth anymore were on Noah's ark.

      The ark floated on top of the water for many months. When God decided the time was right, He sent a wind over the earth to dry up the water. After awhile, Noah decided to send out a big black bird called a raven to see if it could find dry land. The raven flew around but couldn't find anywhere to land, so the bird returned to Noah.

      Next, Noah tried sending a dove out to see if it could find any dry land. The dove returned to Noah just as the raven had. Noah waited a week and then tried sending out the dove again. This time the dove returned with an olive branch in its mouth. That let Noah know that trees were again growing on earth.

      A week later, Noah sent a dove out again and this time it didn't return. That let Noah know that it would be safe to remove the covering that was on the ark. Then God told Noah to come out of the ark and to let the animals come out as well. The earth was beautiful and green. Everyone was excited to be able to come out of the ark after having lived on it for over a year.

The first thing Noah did when he left the ark was to build an altar to God, thanking Him for bringing him and his family safely through the flood.

God was pleased with Noah's offering. God sent a rainbow as a sign. He promised that He would never again use a flood to destroy all of the living creatures on earth again. Every time you see a rainbow, it will help you to remember God's promise to us.

Lesson:
1. Read the story to your child.
2. Discuss all of the animals that were on the ark.
3. Help your child to create an animal face on their plate by drawing eyes and a mouth.
4. Have your child add yarn, cotton balls (fur) and/or torn paper (scales) to your animal creation. Let your child color their picture.
5. Remind your child that God took care of Noah and the animals while they were on the ark and He will also take care of us.

Lesson Seventeen – Noah's Ark

Materials: NIrV Bible – Genesis 6:9 – 8:20
                Cork (from craft store)
                Thumbtacks
                Scissors
                Paper
                Contact Paper
                Crayons or Markers

Preparation: Cut a deep slit in the side of the cork.

Lesson:
1. Read the story of Noah's Ark with your child.
2. Discuss with your child how God protected Noah's family and the animals and He will protect us as well.
3. Help your child to draw a picture of their favorite animal.
4. Help your child to cut out their animal, leaving a tab on the bottom of the animal that is wide enough to fit into the slit on the cork.
5. Use the contact paper to cover the front and back of the animal.
6. Put the animal into the cork slit.
7. Insert a thumbtack on the bottom side of the cork to keep it balanced.

Lesson Eighteen – A Basket Full of Baby

Materials: Play-Doh
                Large Bowl of Water

Preparation: None

Story:

A long time ago in the land of Egypt there was a mean Pharaoh who ruled the land. He was cruel to God's people, who were his slaves. Pharaoh even decided he didn't want any more baby boys to be born to God's people and he gave an order to have them killed as soon as they were born.

God saw the way Pharaoh treated his people and He protected them. One day, one of the families who loved God had a baby boy. This family hid their baby from Pharaoh. The baby grew bigger and bigger.

When the baby was three months old, he was too big for the mom to be able to hide him anymore. She made a basket out of grass. She covered the basket with tar so that it would float in the water. She put her precious baby boy into the basket and then into the water. The mom had her older daughter watch the basket as it floated down the river.

Before long, Pharaoh's daughter came to the river to take a bath. She saw the basket floating in the water and she sent her servant to go get it for her. When the princess opened the basket, she saw the baby. She decided she wanted to keep the baby boy and raise him as her son.

The baby's sister saw what had happened. She asked the princess if she wanted her to go find a woman to help care for the baby. The princess said "yes", so the baby's sister went home and got her mother.

The princess named the baby Moses because she had gotten him out of the water. God had protected the boy as a baby and He protected him as he grew to be a man. God planned to use Moses to help protect the rest of God's people, too.

Lesson:
1. Read the story to your child.
2. Help your child to make a small basket with the play-doh.
3. Help your child make a baby out of the play-doh.
4. Have your child place the baby in the basket and then place the basket into the bowl of water.
5. See if the basket will float or sink.
6. Take them out of the water and let them dry off before you put them away.
7. Remind your child that if God can take care of a baby in a basket, then He can certainly keep them safe as well.

Lesson Nineteen – Baby Moses

Materials: NIrV Bible – Exodus 2:1-10
                    6 Household Items (i.e., Plastic Spoon, Rock, Candy, Button, etc.)

Preparation: Hide the household items around the house.

Lesson:
1. Read the story of baby Moses with your child.
2. Talk about how Moses' family hid him to try to keep him from being found. Explain to your child that God protected Moses even after he was found by Pharaoh's daughter.
3. Have your child try to find the items that you have hidden.

Lesson Twenty – Moses Crosses the Red Sea

Materials: Brown Construction Paper
                    Blue Construction Paper
                    Scissors
                    Glue

Preparation: None

Story:

Pharaoh was still being mean to God's people when Moses grew to be a man. God decided it was time to get His people out of Egypt. God made many bad things called plagues happen to Pharaoh's people to cause them to let God's people go.

As God's people were leaving Egypt, they didn't know which way to go. So God led them out of Egypt. God didn't lead His people down the easiest road. He took them through the hot desert to a big sea called the Red Sea.

God led them with a big cloud during the day and a pillar of fire during the night. The cloud helped to shade the people from the heat of the desert during the day. The fire helped to warm the people from the cold during the night. God was still taking care of His people.

After God's people had left Egypt, Pharaoh changed his mind. He decided he wanted to have God's people back as his slaves. So Pharaoh sent his best men and chariots to chase after the people and bring them back. Pharaoh was sure that his army would be able to force the people to come back; but, he was wrong.

When God's people looked up and saw the chariots coming after them, they were scared. Moses told the people that God would help them and protect them. God's people were trapped between the Red Sea and Pharaoh's army. They began to panic because there was no way for them to escape.

Suddenly, God told Moses to lift his staff. A great wind began to blow. It separated the water into two walls. Between the walls was a dry walkway. All God's people walked through the water on dry land!

An angel of God moved behind the people and protected them from the king's army. God made it dark on the king's side making it hard for them to travel in the darkness. God made it light on the side of God's people as they were traveling through the sea.

When all of God's people got to the other side of the sea, God told Moses to stretch out his hand over the waters. Suddenly the waters closed. All of Pharaoh's army was caught in the water and they drowned.

God took care of His people. They were so excited that they began singing songs to God to thank Him for saving them from the evil pharaoh.

Lesson:
1. Read the story to your child.
2. Lay the blue paper on top of the brown paper.
3. Glue the papers together, leaving about 3 inches in the center with no glue.
4. Cut the blue paper from top to bottom.
5. Help your child to fold up the cut edges of the blue paper.
6. Your child will now have a dry path through the blue water.
7. Let them walk their fingers across on dry ground to reenact the story.
8. Remind your child that God was strong enough to take care of the God's people and that He is strong enough to take care of us as well.

Lesson Twenty-One – Walking Through on Dry Land

Materials: NIrV Bible – Exodus 14:10-31
                 9x11 Baking Pan
                 Tongue Depressor
                 Piece of Transparent Glass the width of the Baking Pan

Preparation: Fill the pan about halfway with water.

Lesson:
1. Read the story of Moses and the Red Sea with your child.
2. Ask your child to try to hold back the water.
3. Give your child the tongue depressor and let them try again.
4. Put the transparent glass into the water. Show them how the glass forms a wall that holds back the water.
5. Ask your child if a man could hold back the water without some kind of wall. Discuss with them how people have to build huge concrete dams to hold back water.
6. Discuss with your child how God was able to push the water into walls with his huge power and didn't have to build a dam or anything else in order to hold the water back.

Lesson Twenty-Two – I'm Hungry

Materials: Bread

                 Paper Lunch Bag

Preparation: Bread the bread up into small pieces and then sprinkle the pieces onto a table.

Story:

       After coming through the Red Sea, God's people wandered around in the desert. The people were starting to get hungry and tired. They complained to Moses about how they didn't have as much food now as they had when they were slaves in Egypt!

       God heard the people complaining and He told Moses that He would rain bread down from heaven for the people. This special bread was called manna. God told them to go out every morning and gather just enough manna for their family to eat that day.

       The next morning, there was a layer of dew on the ground around the camp. When the dew was gone, thin flakes like frost appeared on the desert floor. When God's people saw it, they asked Moses what it was because they didn't know.

       Moses explained to them that it was the bread that God had given for them to eat. God's people gathered the manna as they had been instructed. The manna was another way the God provided for His people when they were in the desert.

Lesson:
1. Read the story to your child.
2. Pretend with your child that you are gathering manna.
3. Have your child fill their lunch bag with the manna.
4. Then let your child eat the manna as part of their lunch or snack.
5. Discuss with your child how God provides all of the food that we eat – that we buy it, but God is the one who provides our job so that we can buy the food. And He is the one who makes it rain so that there is food to buy.

Lesson Twenty-Three – Gathering Manna

Materials: NIrV Bible – Exodus 16:4-17
                        Paper
                        Pencil or Pen

Preparation: None

Lesson:
1. Read the story of gathering manna with your child.
2. Have your child pretend that they are lost in the wilderness. Have them pretend that they have been without food for several days.
3. Ask your child if they could get to a grocery store at that point, what would they buy?
4. Write down the foods that your child mentions.
5. Discuss with your child which of these foods are healthy and are needed by your body and which ones are junk foods.
6. Talk to you child about how God sent the Israelites the perfect food and that He knew just how much to send. Emphasize how God provided for their needs and He also provides for our needs.

Lesson Twenty-Four – All Fall Down

Materials: Blocks

Preparation: None

Story:

A long time ago, God was leading His people into a wonderful land that He had promised to give them. There were already people living in this land – but these people worshipped fake gods and not the One True God.

God was planning to have His people come into the land that He had promised to them and take it over from the people who worshipped the fake gods. God's army would attack the cities and take them over. The first city they were going to attack was called Jericho.

The people of Jericho knew that God's people were coming, so they closed their city gate. The gate was attached to a wall that went around their city. The wall was tall and wide. The people were confident that no one could get past that wall and into their city.

The leader of God's people at this time was named Joshua. God spoke to Joshua and told him that He had a plan to help His people get into the city. God wanted Joshua's army to march around the city one time every day for six days. Then, on the seventh day, God wanted them to march around the city seven times. God wanted the priests to blow trumpets, but to have everyone else be quiet.

God's people obeyed. They marched around the city one time every day for six days and then marched back to camp. The people of Jericho were probably laughing at them. God's army kept marching around their city but they didn't even try to get through the wall.

On the seventh day, God's army marched around the city seven times. The priests blew a long blast on their trumpets and the rest of the army shouted! All of the sudden everyone heard a loud, rumbling sound. The walls of Jericho were falling down! God had opened the city walls for His army. God's army went in and took over the city.

Isn't that an amazing story?!? Remember, God's people had to believe what God said and do what He said to do for it to work. The people obeyed God's instructions, even though it probably didn't make sense to them. They followed God's instructions exactly and everything turned out just right.

When we follow God's instructions in the Bible, things will work out for us, too. We may not get everything we want; but, God tells us that He will take care of His people. And when God makes a promise you can be sure that He will keep it.

Lesson:
1. Read the story to your child.
2. Help your child to build a big tower with their blocks.
3. Now pretend that you are Joshua and the Israelites (God's people).
4. March around the tower. Then shout and knock the blocks down.
5. Do this over and over as long as your child is interested.

6. Discuss with your child who actually knocked down the walls of Jericho – that it was God and not the Israelites. Talk to them about how God was doing this to give the Israelites somewhere to live now that they weren't in Egypt any longer.

Lesson Twenty-Five – Jericho Falls Down

Materials: NIrV Bible – Joshua 6:1-20
               Popcorn (can get colored for more effect)

Preparation: None

Lesson:
1. Read the story of Jericho with your child.
2. Show your child some unpopped kernels.
3. Discuss how the kernels are like people. Without heat, these kernels just lie there. But when you add heat, the energy released from that heat causes them to change into something pretty and tasty.
4. Pop the popcorn.
5. While it's popping, discuss with your child how without Jesus we're like these plain kernels. Only as we come to know Him better will we see all of the great things He has done for us. Only as we spend more time with Him will we understand the awesome things He wants to do for us.
6. Discuss how as we allow Jesus to be in charge of our lives, we will explode with joy. We will be so filled with thankfulness and amazement at God's goodness that we will want to share the joy with others.
7. Enjoy the popcorn treat with your child.

Lesson Twenty-Six – The 23rd Psalm

Materials: NIrV Bible – Psalm 23
               Pancake Mix (can make from scratch or using Bisquick)
               Butter
               Maple Syrup

Preparation: None

Lesson:
1. Read the 23rd Psalm to your child.
2. Discuss how God wants to take care of us with your child.
3. Let your child help you mix the pancake batter.
4. Make sheep-shaped pancakes and enjoy them with your child.

Lesson Twenty-Seven – Daniel in the Lion's Den

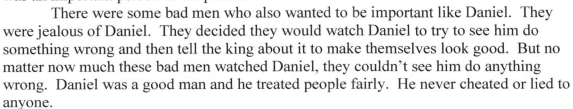

Materials: None

Preparation: None

Story:

     Daniel was a man who loved God very much. He prayed to God three times every day. Daniel was friends with his king and he was an important person in the palace.

     There were some bad men who also wanted to be important like Daniel. They were jealous of Daniel. They decided they would watch Daniel to try to see him do something wrong and then tell the king about it to make themselves look good. But no matter now much these bad men watched Daniel, they couldn't see him do anything wrong. Daniel was a good man and he treated people fairly. He never cheated or lied to anyone.

     The men couldn't find anything wrong with Daniel. They did notice that Daniel loved God and prayed to Him three times a day. Suddenly, these bad men had a sneaky idea. They talked to the king and convinced him that everyone should only pray to the king and to no one else. The king thought it was a good idea, so he made it a law that people could only pray to him.

     Daniel heard about the king's new law. Daniel knew that he worshipped the One True God, though, and he must only pray to Him. So Daniel went back to his house and prayed by the window. The bad men were watching Daniel and saw him pray to God.

     The bad men ran back to the king and told him about Daniel. The king was sad because Daniel was his friend. The king tried to find a way to save Daniel, but he couldn't think of anything that he could do.

     Daniel's punishment was to be put into a lion's den. These lions were very hungry and would eat up anything that was thrown into their den. The king talked to Daniel and told him that he hoped Daniel's God would rescue him. They threw Daniel into the den and put a big stone in front of the door.

     The king was upset! He went back to the palace and he couldn't eat or sleep because he was so worried about Daniel.

     The next morning, the king ran to check on Daniel. He yelled, "Daniel, did your God rescue you?!?"

Daniel said, "Yes, He did!"

     They pulled Daniel out of the den and everyone saw that he did not even have a scratch on him. Through the night, God had sent an angel to shut all of the lions' mouths. They couldn't eat Daniel. God had kept Daniel safe the whole night long.

     The king thanked God for saving Daniel. This made the king realize that Daniel's God was real and powerful. From then on, the king and his people worshipped only the One True God, the maker of Heaven and Earth.

Lesson:
1. Read the story to your child.
2. Have your child roar like a lion.
3. Pretend that you are an angel. As soon as you touch the lion's mouth, have your child stop roaring.
4. Now change places with your child – you act like the lion and have your child be the angel.
5. Discuss with your child how God protected Daniel among the lions. Remind your child that God was strong enough to take care of Daniel and that He is also strong enough to take care of us.

Lesson Twenty-Eight – Lions Have Sharp Teeth

Materials: NIrV Bible – Daniel 6:1-24
               Large Appliance Box OR Closet OR Dark Blankets to make a Fort
               Small Flashlight

Preparation: Construct the makeshift fort or prepare the box or closet.

Lesson:
1. Sit inside the box/closet/fort with your child. Make it as dark in there as possible.
2. Ask your child if they can see anything. Ask if they can imagine a place any darker than this one. Ask how long they would like to sit in here.
3. Read the story of Daniel and the Lion's Den to your child – use the flashlight to be able to see the text.
4. Discuss with your child some things that they can do to feel better when they are scared. Talk about how God kept Daniel safe and how He wants to keep us safe as well.

Lesson Twenty-Nine – I Don't Need to Worry

Materials: NIrV Bible – Luke 12:4-7
               Cereal

Preparation: None

Lesson:
1. Read the text to your child.
2. Pretend that you and your child are birds. Flap your wings and say "tweet, tweet."
3. Eat some cereal and pretend that it is birdseed.
4. Discuss with your child how God takes care of the birds and they don't have to worry about where their next meal is coming from.
5. Tell your child we should trust God for our needs as do the birds.

Lesson Thirty – Sandcastles

Materials: NIrV Bible – Luke 6:47-49
Sandbox and Bucket of Water (optional)

Preparation: None

Lesson:
1. Read the parable to your child.
2. Pretend you are a house on the sand. The rain comes down and the wind blows… and you fall down.
3. Now pretend that you are a house on the rock. The rain comes down and the wind blows… and you stay standing.
4. Explain to your child that being a house on a rock is what it's like to be safe in Jesus' arms. That if we obey Jesus and do what He wants us to, we are being like the wise man.
5. Sing "The Wise Man and The Foolish Man" with your child.
6. Optionally, you can build a sandcastle with your child and show them how it falls down when you throw water at it.

The Wise Man and the Foolish Man

The wise man built his house upon the rock,
The wise man built his house upon the rock,
The wise man built his house upon the rock,
And the rains came tumbling down!

The rains came down and the floods came up,
The rains came down and the floods came up,
The rains came down and the floods came up,
And the house on the rock stood firm.

The foolish man built his house upon the sand,
The foolish man built his house upon the sand,
The foolish man built his house upon the sand,
And the rains came tumbling down!

The rains came down and the floods came up,
The rains came down and the floods came up,
The rains came down and the floods came up,
And the house on the sand went SPLAT!

So build your life on the Lord Jesus Christ,
So build your life on the Lord Jesus Christ,
So build your life on the Lord Jesus Christ,
And the blessings will come tumbling down.

The blessings will come down as the prayers go up,
The blessings will come down as the prayers go up,
The blessings will come down as the prayers go up,
So build your life on the Lord!

Lesson Thirty-One – When I'm Afraid

Materials: Empty Jar with Screw-on lid
               Water
               Vegetable Oil
               Food Coloring

Preparation: None

Story:

One day, Jesus and His disciples decided to go to the other side of the lake. They got into a boat and set sail. Once they were in the boat, Jesus fell asleep.

A huge storm came up suddenly and started filling the boat with water. The waves were crashing, the wind was blowing and the rain was pouring down. They were in great danger!

The disciples were terrified. They woke Jesus up and said, "Master, Master, we're going to drown!"

Jesus stood up. He said, "Be still."

The wind stopped blowing. The waves stopped crashing. The storm completely stopped and everything was suddenly calm.

Jesus was disappointed in their fear. He wished that they had trusted Him to take care of them. "Where is your faith?" He asked His disciples.

The disciples were completely amazed that even the winds and the waves obeyed Jesus.

Lesson:
1. Read the story to your child.
2. Help your child to fill the jar half full of water.
3. Help them to fill the rest of the jar with vegetable oil.
4. Help them to add a few drops of food coloring.
5. Put on the lid for your child.
6. Let your child shake the jar hard for stormy waves or shake it gently to make small waves.
7. Remind your child that Jesus took care of the disciples during the storm and He also wants to take care of us.

Lesson Thirty-Two – Wow, Where'd the Storm Go?!?

Materials: NIrV Bible – Luke 8:22-25
              Thin Cookie Sheet
              Wooden Spoon
              Pots and Pans
              Spray Bottle filled with Water
              Fan

Preparation: None

Lesson:
1. Read the story of Jesus calming the storm to your child.
2. Give your child a cookie sheet. Let them shake it to make a thunder noise.
3. Give your child a pan and a wooden spoon to beat on them.
4. Let your child spray the spray bottle.
5. Work the fan and the lights.
6. Re-enact the story with all of these effects. Remind your child to stop everything when Jesus calms the storm.

Lesson Thirty-Three – The Fiery Furnace

Materials: Orange Jell-o
                      Red Jell-o
                      Spray Whipped Cream

Preparation: Make orange and red Jell-o Jigglers as the "fire" for snack. The recipe is on the back of the package.

Story:

Long ago, in Babylon, there lived three men who loved God very much. Their names were Shadrach, Meshach, and Abednego. These men were important people and they worked for their king.

The king of Babylon did not love God. One day the king decided to make a huge golden statue. It was enormous! The king ordered everyone to bow down and worship the statue. The king made a law that if anyone did not bow down to the statue, they would be thrown into a hot, fiery furnace.

Shadrach, Meshach and Abednego knew that the statue wasn't the One True God and they would not bow down to worship a fake god. Some leaders saw that they did not obey the king's new law. They told the king.

The king was furious! He could not believe that they would not bow down to worship the statue. He had Shadrach, Meshach and Abednego brought into the palace. The king asked them if it was true that they didn't bow down to the statue. He said, "I'll give you another chance. If you will bow down now, nothing bad will happen to you. But if you don't, then we'll see if your God can save you!"

The three men replied to the king, "King, our God whom we serve is able to save us and He will rescue us from you. But, even if He doesn't, we want you to know that we will not worship your fake god."

Oh, did that ever make the king angry! He ordered his men to heat the furnace seven times hotter than normal. He commanded the strongest men in the army to tie up Shadrach, Meshach and Abednego and throw them in. The soldiers grabbed the men and dragged them to the furnace. The fire was so hot that it killed the soldiers on the way there and Shadrach, Meshach and Abednego fell into the furnace.

Suddenly the king rubbed his eyes. "What!?!" He said, "Didn't we throw three men into the fire?!? I can see four people in there. The three are not tied with rope and the fourth looks like the Son of God." The king also noticed that the men were not on fire.

The king went to the opening of the furnace and shouted, "Shadrach, Meshach and Abednego, come out!"

So the men came out. And do you know what?!? They weren't burned at all, their hair wasn't singed, and they didn't even smell like smoke!

The king praised God. He now knew that their God was the One and Only True God.

Lesson:
1. Read the story to your child.
2. Discuss with your child how God took care of the three men even when they were inside the furnace – and if He's powerful enough to do that, He's certainly powerful enough to take care of us.
3. Help your child to spray whipped cream on their "fire" snack to put out the flames.
4. Enjoy the snack with your child.

Lesson Thirty-Four – What Should I Do?!?

Materials: NIrV Bible - Daniel 3:1-30
                 Popsicle Stick
                 Cardstock
                 Red and Green Crayons
                 Marker
                 Glue

Preparation:
1. Cut a large circle from the cardstock (4-5" diameter)
2. Using the marker, print a large NO on one side of the circle and a large YES on the other side.

Lesson:
1. Read the story of the Fiery Furnace to your child.
2. Let your child color their circles (red on the no side – green on the yes side.)
3. Help your child to glue their circle onto the popsicle stick.
4. Discuss how Shadrach, Meshach and Abednego had to decide whether or not they should obey the king.
5. Give your child some situations and have them decide whether or not it is something they will do. Have them hold up their yes/no sign to answer you.
   a. Your friend asks you to lie to your Sunday School teacher about something they did.
   b. You're visiting some friends of your mom and dad and they want you to eat things that you know your parents don't want you to eat.
   c. Your sister wants to play with one of your favorite toys – should you share?
   d. Your mom will need help bringing the groceries into the house but you'd rather start playing right away. Should you help your mom first?
   e. Your brother wants you to sneak some cookies from the kitchen without your mom knowing.
   f. Your sister wants you to take a candy bar from the store without paying for it.

Lesson Thirty-Five – Jesus Goes Fishing

Materials: NIrV Bible – John 21:1-14
Dowel Rod or Plastic Spoon
Fish (see companion download)
Yarn or String
Paperclips
Magnets
Fish Picture (see companion download)

Preparation:
1. Print several fish from the companion download. Cut them out.
2. Attach the paperclips to the fish near where their mouths would be.
3. Tie a magnet to one end of a piece of string and a dowel rod to the other end of the string to make the fishing pole.

Lesson:
1. Read the story to your child.
2. Tell your child that fishermen can use nets or poles to catch fish – but today they will be using a pole.
3. Spread the fish out on the floor.
4. Let your child try to catch as many fish as they can with their magnetic fishing pole.

Lesson Thirty-Six – Peter in Prison

Materials: NIrV Bible – Acts 12:1-19
Black Construction Paper
Glue or Tape

Preparation: Cut several strips of construction paper that are approximately five inches long and one inch wide.

Lesson:
1. Read the story to your child.
2. Help your child to connect several of the strips together to make a chain.
3. Fasten the last circle on each end around your child's wrists.
4. Read the story to your child again.
5. When you read the part of the story where the chains fell off of Peter's arms, have your child break the chains around their wrists.
6. Discuss with your child how God was powerful enough to break Peter out of prison and He's powerful enough to take care of us, too.

Lesson Thirty-Seven – You're a Star

Materials: Aluminum Foil
                      String or Yarn
                      Star Stickers
                      Hole Punch

Preparation: None

Story:

      One day, God talked to a man named Abraham. God told Abraham to move away from his family and friends. Abraham loved God and listened to Him. God also told Abraham that he would have many children and grandchildren. He told Abraham that He would bless him and protect him.

      Abraham obeyed God and traveled where God told him to go. Abraham took his wife, Sarah, his nephew, Lot, and everything they owned with him.

      Abraham and his family lived in tents. So, every time God told them to move, they had to roll up their tents and travel. It was lots of work, but they obeyed God and did what He said.

      God kept His promise and protected Abraham.

Lesson:
1. Read the story to your child.
2. Discuss with your child how God took care of Abraham and his descendants and kept them safe – and how He also wants to keep us safe.
3. Give your child several pieces of aluminum foil.
4. Let your child crumple and flatten the foil to create star shapes.
5. Punch a hole at the top of each star.
6. Thread the string through each hole and hang the stars from your child's ceiling at varying heights.
7. Seeing the stars in their room will help your child to remember that God keeps His promises to us just as He did to Abraham.

Lesson Thirty-Eight – Follow the Footprints

Materials: NIrV Bible – Genesis 12:1-9
                       Brown Paper Grocery Sacks
                       A Marker

Preparation: None

Lesson:
1. Read the story to your child.
2. Trace your child's feet onto the grocery sacks several times.
3. Help your child to cut out the footprints.
4. Have your child hide their eyes while you make a path through the house.
5. Let your child follow the footprints to find you.
6. Explain to your child how Abraham followed God's instructions even when he didn't know where God would lead him. Talk about how God took care of Abraham and kept him safe on his journey – and He also wants to keep us safe.

Lesson Thirty-Nine – Sleeping in Tents

Materials: Graham Crackers
                       Marshmallow Cream
                       Plastic Knives

Preparation: None

Story:

      Abraham and his nephew, Lot, traveled around the desert in tents. They followed God and did what He said to do. Abraham had many sheep and other animals. They traveled with them and grazed on the land. Lot also had many animals. As the large group moved from place to place, they had to have enough land for both groups of animals to graze.

      As the animal herds and flocks grew, they needed more food and land for their animals. Food for the animals was getting harder and harder to find. Lots' shepherds started arguing with Abraham's shepherds. They argued over whose animals would get to eat the grass.

      Abraham said, "Let's not have any quarreling between my shepherds and your shepherds because we are family. There is a lot of land around us. Maybe we should separate. If you go to the left, I will go to the right. If you go to the right, I will go to the left."

      Lot looked up and saw the beautiful green grass around the river. He also saw two cities that had lots of activity. So Lot chose for himself the green pastureland to the east. Because Lot chose this land, Abraham went to the west and settled in the land of Canaan.

Lot lived near a city called Sodom. It was full of activity, but the people were wicked and mean. They often made bad choices and sinned against God.

Lot chose to be around people who did wrong and it caused him and his family to accept the sin. They probably did more wrong things because they were around other people who sinned.

Abraham chose to follow God and obey Him. He did right things and lived to please God.

God continued to tell Abraham that He would protect him and give him many children. God told Abraham to look all around. God promised Abraham that He would give his family all of the land that he could see. Abraham believed God and knew He would keep His promise.

Lesson:
1. Read the story to your child.
2. Help your child to lay one graham cracker flat on the table.
3. Then let them spread marshmallow cream onto two other crackers and lean them together to make a tent shape.
4. Explain to your child that Abraham and Sarah traveled and lived in tents much of their lives. Discuss how God kept Abraham and Sarah safe in their tent – and He can certainly keep us safe in our house. God also provided plenty of food for Abraham's animals.
5. Let your child enjoy eating their tent snack.

What God Has Done
God Created Everything

Lesson Forty – God Made the World

Materials: None

Preparation: None

Story:

    The first book in the Bible is called Genesis. The word Genesis means "beginning." We are going to learn about how God created the world. Do you know what it means to create? It means to make something out of nothing. Only God can create. We can make things out of mud or play-doh or paper… but only God can take nothing and make it into something. He is so powerful He can just speak and things will happen. So, this is how God created our beautiful world.

    On the first day, God created the heavens and the earth. The earth was empty. God created light, which He called day and dark which He called night.

    On the second day, God separated the waters from the waters. That means He made the sky. The entire earth was covered with water.

    On the third day, God created land, plants, rocks and trees.

    On the fourth day, God created the sun to light the day and the moon and stars to light the night.

    On the fifth day, God created the birds to fly above the earth. He also created the fish to swim in the sea.

    On the sixth day, God created animals that live on the land. God also made people on the sixth day. God looked at everything that He had created and He smiled – He knew it was good.

    On the seventh day, God rested. God does not get tired like we do. He did this to show us that we should also work six days a week but should rest on the seventh day.

    This is also why we have seven days in each week. Did you know that God is the one who showed us how many days to have in a week?!? He is powerful and He tells us how to do things in order to take care of us. God loves us very much and He always wants what's best for us!

Lesson:
1. Read the story to your child.
2. Go back and forth with your child naming things that God made when He created the world.

Lesson Forty-One – God Made Everything

Materials: NIrV Bible – Genesis 1:1 – 2:3
                 Small Flower Pot
                 Seeds or a Seedling Plant
                 Potting Soil
                 Cup for Watering

Preparation: None

Lesson:
1. Read the creation story to your child.
2. Help your child to plant the seeds or the young plant in the flower pot. Be sure to let your child do the majority of the work.
3. Over the next few weeks, let your child watch their plant grow.
4. Help your child to pray and thank God for all of the wonderful plants that He has created.

Lesson Forty-Two – A Tasty World

Materials: NIrV Bible – Genesis 2:4-17
                 A Variety of Foods (i.e., Broccoli, Carrots, Pretzels, Licorice, Nuts & seeds)
                 Blue or Green Paper Plates

Preparation: None

Lesson:
1. Read the story to your child.
2. Challenge your child to create a colorful world. They may want to build broccoli trees, licorice snakes, or a carrot sun.
3. Discuss with your child the wonderful and tasty foods that God created when He made our world.

Lesson Forty-Three – Lots of Animals

Materials: NIrV Bible – Genesis 2:19-20
                Ink Pad
                Markers or Crayons
                Paper

Preparation: None

Lesson:
1. Read the story to your child.
2. Using the ink, take turns with your child putting your fingerprints on the paper.
3. Point out to your child that everyone has unique fingerprints. No two people's fingerprints are the same – just as all of the people God has created are also unique.
4. Use the markers or crayons to add ears, noses, etc. to create a variety of unique animal prints.
5. Discuss with your child about the wonderful variety of animals in creation that display God's amazing creativity.
6. Talk about how God let Adam name all of the animals. Name as many different kinds of animals as you and your child can think of.
7. Make up names for your fingerprint animal creations.

What God Has Done
God Created You

Lesson Forty-Four – Sweet Reminders

Materials: NIrV Bible – Genesis 2:20b-24
                     Powdered Sugar
                     Peanut Butter
                     Raisins, Seeds and/or Chocolate Sprinkles

Preparation:
1. Mix equal parts of powdered sugar and peanut butter together.
2. Knead the mixture to form a soft dough.

Lesson:
1. Read the story to your child.
2. Give your child a small handful of the dough and tell them to make a dough person.
3. Let your child use the raisins, seeds or chocolate sprinkles to make eyes, bellybuttons, freckles and hair.
4. Discuss with your child how God created us in His image. Talk about the difference between creating (making something out of nothing) and making a person out of dough. Ask your child if God used dough to make us.
5. Have your child tell you about his person.
6. Enjoy the sweet treats with your child.

Lesson Forty-Five – I'm a Present

Materials: NIrV Bible - Psalm 127:3-5

Preparation: None

Lesson:
1. Read the story to your child.
2. Sing the "Happy Birthday" song with your child.
3. Discuss how God made you and how grateful you are that He gave him or her to you to raise.

<u>Happy Birthday</u>
Happy Birthday to you,
Happy Birthday to you,
Happy Birthday dear Adam,
Happy Birthday to you.

Lesson Forty-Six – God Made Me

Materials: NIrV Bible – Genesis 1:26-30

Preparation: None

Lesson:
1. Read the story to your child.
2. Sing the "Head, Shoulders, Knees and Toes" song.
3. Discuss how special your child is – and remind them that God created him or her in His image.

Head, Shoulders, Knees and Toes
Head, Shoulders, Knees and Toes, Knees and Toes,
Head, Shoulders, Knees and Toes, Knees and Toes,
Eyes and Ears and Mouth and Nose,
Head, Shoulders, Knees and Toes, Knees and Toes.

(point to body parts as you say their names)

Lesson Forty-Seven – I Wish I Were Taller

Materials: Zacchaeus (see companion download)
                    Leaves (see companion download)
                    Tree (see companion download)
                    Glue

Preparation:
1. Print the picture of Zacchaeus from the companion download and cut him out.
2. Print several copies of the leaves from the companion download and cut them out.
3. Print the tree from the companion download.

Story:

Jesus was preaching and teaching people. As He walked along the road, He passed through the town of a man named Zacchaeus. Zacchaeus was a tax collector and he was rich. Zacchaeus wanted to see Jesus; but, a crowd of people was following Him around and Zacchaeus was too short to see over all of the people. So he ran ahead and climbed a sycamore tree. He did this so he would be high enough to see Jesus when He passed by him.

When Jesus reached the tree, He looked up and said, "Zacchaeus, come down right away. I must stay at your house today." So Zacchaeus came down at once and welcomed Jesus gladly.

The crowd of people saw this and began to complain. "He is going to eat with a bad man!" You see, Zacchaeus used to force people to pay more tax money than they owed. So the people did not like Zacchaeus.

Zacchaeus had a change of heart when he stood before Jesus. He said, "Look, Lord. Right now, I will give half of everything I own to the poor. And I will pay back everyone I have cheated four times more than what I took from them."

Jesus could tell that Zacchaeus was repenting of his wicked ways. He was turning his back on the naughty things he used to do and was going to start doing what God wanted him to do instead.

Zacchaeus must have also believed that Jesus was the Son of God and trusted Him to be his Savior because Jesus said, "Today salvation has come to this house."

Lesson:
1. Read the story of Zacchaeus to your child.
2. Remind your child that God created us in His image and we are all special. Zacchaeus was shorter than he wanted to be but he didn't let that stop him from seeing Jesus. If your child is unhappy with something about themselves, remind them that we need to try to be content with how God has made us.
3. Help your child to glue the leaves onto the tree. Be sure to leave one part of each leaf loose.
4. Take turns hiding Zacchaeus under one of the leaves and see if the other one can find him.

Lesson Forty-Eight – David will be a King

Materials: Picture of an x-ray (see companion download)

Preparation: Print the x-ray from the companion download.

Story:

        Samuel was a good man who loved God. He was a prophet, which means that he would bring people messages from God.
        One day, God told Samuel that He wanted him to go to Bethlehem. God had chosen who would be the next king and He was going to show him to Samuel. God told him that the next king would be the son of a man named Jesse. Samuel obeyed God and went to Bethlehem.
        When he arrived, Samuel saw one of the sons of Jesse named Eliab. Samuel saw how tall and handsome he was and thought that surely he would be the new king. But God said to Samuel, "I have rejected him. I don't look at the outside appearance, I look at their heart."
        So Jesse brought one of his younger sons to Samuel. Samuel said, "The Lord has not chosen this one, either." Jesse continued to bring his sons to Samuel one by one, but each time Samuel knew that this wasn't the right son.
        After Samuel had seen seven of Jesse's sons, he said, "The Lord has not chosen these. Are these all of the sons you have?"
        "No," said Jesse, "You haven't seen my youngest son, David, but he is out tending the sheep."
        Samuel said, "Bring him to me."
        So Jesse had his youngest son brought to Samuel. Jesse hadn't even considered his youngest son. When David entered the room, Samuel said, "He is the one the Lord has chosen. David will be the new king."

Lesson:
  1. Read the story of David to your child.
  2. Show your child the x-ray picture from the companion download.
  3. Discuss with your child how sometimes we look just fine on the outside; but, on the inside there is something wrong, like a broken bone. A doctor can take an x-ray of us and see what's actually wrong on the inside to help us get well.
  4. Talk about how God does the same thing. He looks inside at our heart. Tell your child that Samuel couldn't tell which of Jesse's sons would have been the best new king by looking at the outside – but God could tell by looking at the inside.
  5. Talk about how God created us and He knows us better and loves us more than anyone else.

What God Has Done
God Gave Us the Bible

Lesson Forty-Nine – The Bible is God's Word

Materials: NIrV Bible – 2 Peter 1:21
                      Graham Crackers
                      Frosting
                      Red Licorice Whips
                      Plastic Knife or Cheese Spreader

Preparation: None

Lesson:
1. Read the verse to your child.
2. Tell your child that every word in the Bible is true. The Bible was written by "holy men who were taught by the Holy Spirit."
3. Explain that it means that every word in the Bible is exactly the way God wants it to be. The Bible is like an instruction manual from God for us – to help us to know how we should act here on earth. He is so much wiser than we are. If we are smart, we will listen to God's wise directions for our lives.
4. Help your child to make a "Bible" snack. Let them frost two graham crackers.
5. Have them lay a licorice whip across one edge of the graham cracker.
6. Put the frosted sides of the crackers together. The crackers are the covers of their Bible and the frosting is the pages. The licorice whip is their page marker.
7. Let your child enjoy their Bible snack.

Lesson Fifty – The Lord is my Lighthouse

Materials: NIrV Bible – Psalm 119:97-105

Preparation: None

Lesson:
1. Read the psalm to your child.
2. Take your child to an interior room such as a bathroom or closet and turn off the light. (NOTE: You may want to have your child sit on your lap or hold your hand while you do this so that they don't become frightened.)
3. Let them experience how dark the room is (with no window and no light.)
4. Now turn on the light.
5. Discuss with your child how it's easier to see when the light is on. Explain to your child how God is like that light. It's hard to see what's really going on around us and how to act without God (and God's Word) to explain things to us and to tell us how to act.

Lesson Fifty-One – Read the Bible

Materials: NIrV Bible – Psalm 119:89-93
              Masking Tape

Preparation: Mark an X on the floor with the masking tape.

Lesson:
1. Read the psalm to your child.
2. Have your child stand on the X.
3. Have them cover their eyes with their hands and try to walk in a straight line for five steps.
4. Without uncovering their eyes, have them turn around and walk ahead five steps.
5. Now have them uncover their eyes and look where they're standing. Are they in the same place that they started? Why or why not?
6. Discuss with your child how reading the Bible will help them to get to where they really should be in life and not where they THINK they should be.

Lesson Fifty-Two – Philip and the Chariot

Materials: Construction Paper
              Marker
              String or yarn
              Picture of a Chariot (see companion download)

Preparation:
1. Print the chariot from the companion download.
2. Write "Jesus loves you!" on the paper.

Story:

There once was a man named Philip who had been one of Jesus' disciples. After Jesus went back to heaven, Philip went from town to town telling people that Jesus was the Son of God.

One day, an angel of the Lord told Philip to walk down a desert road that leads from Jerusalem to Gaza. So Philip started walking down the road. On his way, he met an important Ethiopian man in a chariot. (Show your child the picture of the chariot from the companion download.) The man was reading the Bible. God told Philip to walk up to the chariot.

Philip obeyed. He ran up to the chariot and heard the man reading the book of Isaiah, which is part of the Bible. "Do you understand what you are reading?" Philip asked.

"How can I," the man said, "unless someone explains it to me?" So the man invited Philip to come up and sit with him.

The man was reading words that talked about Jesus and how He would come to the world to be our Savior. Philip explained to him the good news about Jesus and how He had died to save us from our sins.

As they traveled along the road, they came to some water. The man wanted to be baptized. He believed that Jesus was the Son of God and he wanted to become a Christian. Philip had used the words of the Bible to be able to tell this man about Jesus.

Lesson:
1. Read the story to your child.
2. Explain to your child that the man in the chariot wasn't reading a Bible like we have today. He was probably reading a scroll.
3. Give your child the construction paper and show them how to make a scroll by rolling the paper into a tube shape.
4. Tie the scroll with the string.
5. Discuss with your child how sometimes it's hard to understand the Bible and we need someone to help explain things to us. Explain how our pastors and teachers help us to understand things better when we're at church.
6. Save the scroll for tomorrow's lesson.

Lesson Fifty-Three – King Josiah Finds the Bible

Materials: Scroll from Yesterday's Lesson

Preparation: None

Story:

One day a long time ago, a little boy became the king. He was only eight years old! This little boy was named Josiah.

When Josiah grew up, he noticed how God's church was dirty and things were broken and run down. He asked his workers to repair the church. The men worked and hammered to fix the church temple. One day, they found something wonderful in a dusty, dirty pile. A man picked up the surprise and brought it to King Josiah.

The surprise was a scroll Bible. This was the only copy of the Bible they had and it had been lost for a long time! They brushed the dust off the Bible and opened it.

When they read the Bible, Josiah called all the people to come and listen to God's words. They listened carefully. They had not heard God's words before. They were heartbroken because God wanted them to be doing some things they hadn't even known about. They hadn't known how God wanted them to act without being able to read the Bible before.

Now that they had the Bible and knew what to do, the people promised to obey God and follow Him with all of their hearts. God was pleased with Josiah and with His people.

Lesson:
1. Read the story to your child.

2. Explain to them that we know what God wants us to do by reading His instructions to us in the Bible.
3. Play hide and seek with the scroll that you made in yesterday's lesson. Pretend that you are Josiah's workmen finding the scroll in the temple.

What God Has Done
God's Son, Jesus, Died for your Sins so that You Can Be With God

Lesson Fifty-Four – A Very Special Baby

Materials: Pre-Made Cookie Dough
             A Rolling Pin
             An Angel-Shaped Cookie Cutter
             A Baking Sheet
             Frosting or other Cookie Decorations

Preparation: None

Story:

The king in those days had decided he wanted to know how many people lived in his land; so, Joseph and Mary had to travel to Bethlehem so they could be counted. It must have been a hard journey for them, because Mary was about to have a baby.

When they arrived in Bethlehem, they looked for somewhere to stay. There were so many people in Bethlehem that they couldn't find any rooms in the inn. The innkeeper was kind enough to let them stay in his stable for the night. While they were there, Mary gave birth to a son. She wrapped the baby in a blanket and put him down to sleep in a manger.

In a nearby field, there were some shepherds who were watching their sheep. It was nighttime and they were sleepy. An angel of the Lord went to them. He was bright and surrounded by the glory of God. When the shepherds saw him, they were terrified.

"Today, in Bethlehem, a special baby has been born, "said the angel. "He is the Son of God."

Suddenly the sky was filled with angels. They were all singing and praising God.

When the angels left, the shepherds said to one another, "Let's go to Bethlehem and see this special baby that God has told us about."

So they hurried to Bethlehem. They found Mary, Joseph, and the baby in the stable. Baby Jesus was still lying in the manger.

The shepherds worshipped the special baby. When they left, they told everyone they met about their amazing night. Everyone they told was amazed at what had happened. God had been promising for many years that He would send His Son to be our Savior and the time had finally come. What a wonderful night!

Lesson:
1. Read the story to your child.
2. Let your child help roll out the cookie dough and cut out some angel-shaped cookies.
3. Bake the cookies.
4. When the cookies are cool, let your child decorate them.
5. Discuss how God must have truly loved us if He would send his Son to Earth to die for us.

6. Discuss with your child how Jesus was a human baby – but he was also still God. This will be a hard concept for your child to fully grasp; but, it is important to start telling them about it so that the seed is planted in their mind.

Lesson Fifty-Five – Jesus is Born

Materials: NIrV Bible – Luke 2:1-20
Picture of a Manger Scene (see companion download)
Picture of Baby Jesus (see companion download)
Tape
Blindfold
Contact Paper (optional)

Preparation:
1. Print the manger scene from the companion download. You may want to cover the picture with contact paper so that your child can have several chances to play the game.
2. Print several copies of the picture of Baby Jesus from the companion download and cut them out for your child.

Lesson:
1. Read the story to your child.
2. Roll a piece of tape onto the back of each picture of Baby Jesus.
3. Play "Pin the Baby Jesus on the Manger" with your child. See how close they can get to the manger.

Lesson Fifty-Six – Keeping Jesus Safe

Materials: Piece of Scrap Wood
              Nails
              Lightweight Hammer

Preparation: None

Story:

After Jesus was born in Bethlehem, some wise men from the east traveled to Jerusalem. They had been following a bright star which told them of Jesus' birth. The wise men asked several people in Jerusalem where the king of the Jews had been born.

King Herod heard what the wise men were asking and he was upset. He didn't want a new king to be born. After all, he was the king! Herod called his closest advisers together and asked them where the Christ was supposed to be born. The advisers told him the baby was to be born in Bethlehem.

Then Herod called the wise men to him to find out exactly when they had first seen the special star. He told them to continue looking for the child. When they found Him, he asked them to come back and tell him so he could go and worship the new king with them.

After the wise men had talked to Herod they continued on their way. They followed the star until they came to the house where Joseph, Mary, and Jesus lived. When they saw Jesus, they bowed down and worshipped Him. Then they brought out treasures and presented them to Jesus as gifts.

God caused the wise men to have a dream which warned them not to tell Herod where Jesus was living. So they returned to their country without going through Jerusalem.

When Herod realized that the wise men weren't going to tell him where the new king was, he decided to kill all the baby boys in Bethlehem who were two years old and under.

God protected His Son from the bad king. He caused Joseph to have a dream warning him to get up during the night and take Jesus to Egypt. Joseph obeyed God. He took his family to Egypt and stayed there until King Herod died.

Joseph was a good father. He knew that Jesus was God's Son, but he treated Him like his son as well. Joseph and Mary raised Jesus to be a good, strong boy who loved and obeyed God.

Lesson:
1. Read the story to your child.
2. Explain to your child that Joseph was a carpenter and that Jesus probably learned how to be a carpenter, too.
3. Hammer the nail part way into the piece of scrap wood.
4. Let your child finish hammering the nail. Be sure they keep their fingers back. You will want to hold the wood for them.

Lesson Fifty-Seven – Jesus Died to Pay for My Sins

Materials: Bathtub

Preparation: None

Story:

God sent Jesus to earth to pay the price for all our sins. We
sin is every time we don't share our toys, or we lie, or we whine to get our way, or
anything else we do that is naughty. Jesus never sinned. Jesus was punished for
everything naughty that everyone on earth had ever done. It is a sad story; but, this is
how it happened.

Jesus was taken prisoner by a group of soldiers. They beat him. Then they took
off his clothes and put a scarlet robe on him. Then they twisted together a crown of
thorns and pushed it onto his head. They put a staff in his right hand and made fun of
him. They called him names. They spit on him and hit him. Remember, Jesus had never
done anything wrong. He was being punished for things that we do wrong.

Jesus was weak from being beaten. They made him carry his cross until he
couldn't do it anymore. Then they had another man named Simon carry it for him.

They came to a place named Golgotha, which is where they were going to kill
Jesus. They nailed him to a cross. This is a horrible way to die – but it is the way that
Romans often killed criminals in those days.

The soldiers made fun of Jesus while he was hanging on the cross. They said that
if he was the Son of God, he should save himself. Jesus could have saved himself. If he
had done that, though, then he wouldn't have taken the punishment for our sins. So,
because he loved us, he obeyed his Father and stayed on the cross.

After several hours on the cross, Jesus died. When he did, darkness covered the
land. There was also a violent earthquake. People came back to life. Many amazing
things happened! The Roman soldiers were terrified and they said, "Surely He was the
Son of God!"

Lesson:
1. Let your child play outside or do something which will cause them to get really
   dirty.
2. Read the story to your child.
3. Have your child take a bath.
4. After they are clean, have them look at the dirty water and imagine that it is their
   sins.
5. Then let the water drain from the tub. Tell them that Jesus is like the water and
   the drain – He takes our sins away.

Lesson Fifty-Eight – Jesus Dies

Materials: NIrV Bible – Matthew 27:27-54
                     Popsicle Sticks
                     Glue
                     Flower Pot
                     Potting Soil

Preparation: None

Lesson:
1. Read the story of Jesus' crucifixion to your child.
2. Help your child to make three crosses out of the popsicle sticks and glue.
3. Let your child fill the flower pot with potting soil.
4. Have them place the three crosses into the dirt.
5. Put the pot where it will be a daily reminder to your child that Jesus died because He loves them.

Lesson Fifty-Nine – The Resurrection

Materials: Red Construction Paper
                     Popsicle Sticks or Brown Construction Paper
                     Glue or Tape

Preparation:
1. Draw a heart on the red construction paper.
2. If you're using brown construction paper rather than popsicle sticks, cut a couple of strips to be used as a cross later.

Story:

       Three days after Jesus had been killed, some women went to see where he had been buried. These women were his friends and they were going to put perfumes on Jesus' body.

       These women got a big surprise! On the way to see Jesus' body, there was a rumbling noise like an earthquake. When the women got to the grave they were shocked! The grave was open and an angel was sitting on the rock.

       Suddenly the angel spoke to the women. The angel told them that Jesus was alive. The women were so excited.

       They ran back to tell all of Jesus' friends the good news. Jesus wasn't dead anymore. He had come back to life, just like he had said he would.

       As they were running, Jesus met them. They hugged him and told him how much they loved him. Jesus told them to keep going to tell his other friends the great news.

       The women obeyed and told everyone the good news. Jesus was alive! We must tell our friends the good news just like the women did.

Lesson:
1. Read the story to your child.
2. Have your child cut out the heart.
3. Help your child to make a cross with the popsicle sticks or the brown construction paper strips.
4. Explain to your child that all people do naughty things and that these things are called sins. Because of sin, we can't live in Heaven with God. But Jesus loves us so much that He died on the cross for our sins. Jesus didn't stay dead, but God brought Him back to life and He lives in Heaven. Everyone who believes in Jesus and tries to obey Him will live in Heaven with God someday.
5. While explaining these concepts to your child, let them fasten the heart to the cross.

Lesson Sixty – Jesus is Alive

Materials: NIrV Bible - Matthew 28:1-10
                 Items which are alive (plant, pet, bug, etc.)
                 Items which are not alive (paper, chair, rock, etc.)

Preparation: None

Lesson:
1. Read the story of Jesus' resurrection to your child.
2. Discuss with your child how God raised Jesus from the dead.
3. Show your child the different items you have collected. Talk to them about what it means to be alive.
4. Help your child to identify which items are alive and which ones are not.

Lesson Sixty-One – Jesus Will Come Back

Materials: A Mystery Snack
                A Lunch Bag

Preparation: Put the snack inside the lunch bag and don't let your child see what it is.

Story:

One day, after Jesus had come back to life, he talked to his friends about what it would be like one day when it was time to go to Heaven.

He shared that He would come down from Heaven and everyone would see him in the clouds. Angels would blow trumpets so loud that everyone in the whole world would know that Jesus was here.

Then, everyone who believed in Jesus would go to Heaven.

It will be a happy time for everyone who believes and trusts in Jesus.

Jesus wanted his friends to know this news so they could tell everyone they know how important it is to believe in Jesus and trust him with all their heart. Jesus wants all people to go to Heaven one day. It is up to each person to choose to love Jesus and follow him. Isn't it exciting to know that one day Jesus will return?!?

Lesson:
1. Make sure your child sees the lunch bag. Try to create drama in that there's a mystery snack inside. Get them excited about it!
2. Read the story to your child.
3. Discuss with your child how Jesus will come back to earth someday and will bring all of the Christians to Heaven with him.
4. Let your child reach into the lunch bag and get their surprise snack. Talk about how mysterious it was. Share how they did not know what they would get until they saw it.
5. Explain how the time of Jesus coming back is a mystery to us also. Help them to know how important it is to follow Jesus now so that we're ready when he returns.

You Can Have a Relationship With God
Prayer is talking to God in Jesus' Name

Lesson Sixty-Two – Praying in Jesus' Name

Materials: None

Preparation: None

Story:

Have you ever heard someone say "in Jesus' name I pray" at the end of their prayer? Do you know why they say that?

One reason is that we know that Jesus wants us to talk to God in his name. He told His disciples to pray this way in the Bible. We know that we should do things God's way and not our own way.

Another reason is that it reminds us to have the right attitude when we are praying to God. If it weren't for Jesus taking the punishment for our sins, we would be separated from God. We wouldn't even be able to talk to God if it weren't for Jesus. So, when we pray in Jesus' name, it helps us to remember how much we depend on Jesus for our salvation.

Remember that praying is talking to God and He wants to hear from us as often as possible.

Lesson:
1. Read the story to your child.
2. Pray with your child. If they do not feel comfortable praying on their own, say a prayer that they can repeat.
3. Try not to have your child memorize prayers – teach them to talk to God from their heart, not using a formula.

Lesson Sixty-Three – God Whispers to Elijah

Materials: Chocolate Muffin
                Teddy Grahams (or other person-like cracker)

Preparation: None

Story:

Elijah was a good man who loved God. King Ahab did not love God. One day he became angry with Elijah and he wanted to kill him. Elijah was afraid. Instead of trusting God, he ran for his life. He ended up running out into the desert to try to hide from King Ahab.

Elijah became tired. He sat down and prayed. God heard Elijah's prayers. He sent an angel to bring Elijah bread to eat and water to drink. Elijah regained his strength enough that he was able to continue traveling for more than a month. Then, when he reached God's special mountain, Elijah went into a cave and fell asleep.

God saw Elijah in the cave. He knew how tired he was and He wanted to help him. He said, "What are you doing here, Elijah?"

Elijah said, "I have worked hard for you, God, but I'm so tired and I feel alone. King Ahab wants to kill me!"

God wanted to encourage Elijah. He said, "Go and stand on the mountain in My presence. I am about to pass by."

Then a great and powerful wind tore the mountains apart and shattered the rocks before the Lord; but, the Lord was not in the wind. After the wind there was an earthquake; but, the Lord was not in the earthquake. After the earthquake came a fire; but, the Lord was not in the fire. After the fire came a gentle whisper. When Elijah heard it, he knew the whisper was God. Elijah pulled his cloak over his face and went out to speak to the Lord.

God encouraged Elijah. He told him to go back home – there were 7,000 other people there who also loved Him and worshipped Him. Elijah wasn't alone! God also told Elijah that He was going to appoint a new king – so Elijah wouldn't have to worry about King Ahab anymore.

Lesson:
1. Read the story to your child.
2. Discuss with your child how God helped Elijah went he was feeling so tired and alone. God helped Elijah to see that He would take care of everything and Elijah didn't need to worry.
3. Tell your child that when they are feeling upset or alone, instead of running away or pouting, we should talk to God and ask for His help. He will encourage us like He encouraged Elijah.
4. Make a snack cave. Help your child to hollow out part of their chocolate muffin.
5. Have them put a Teddy Graham inside their cave to be Elijah.
6. Let your child enjoy their snack.

Lesson Sixty-Four – Hezekiah Prays to God

Materials: Small Ball of Clay or Play-Doh
                      Small Flower Pot
                      Chopstick or Piece of a Dowel Rod
                      Ruler
                      Pencil or Marker
                      Watch

Preparation: None

Story:

Long ago, there was a king named Hezekiah. He became sick and was about to die. A man of God named Isaiah came to talk to the king. Isaiah told the king that God said he was about to die.

Hezekiah was sad. He could have lain there and gotten angry. Instead, he prayed, "Lord, I've always tried to obey you and do what is right. Please remember me!" Then King Hezekiah cried.

God heard Hezekiah's prayer and He saw his tears. God told Isaiah to tell the king that He would go ahead and heal him. Isaiah fixed some medicine for the king and he started to get better.

As he was recovering, Hezekiah asked, "How will I know for sure that I will keep healing?"

God sent the king a sign that He would indeed heal him. God made the sun move backwards in the sky. Can you imagine!?! King Hezekiah watched the shadows move backwards and he knew that God would continue to heal him.

Lesson:
1. Read the story to your child.
2. Discuss with your child how Hezekiah had a special prayer request he wanted God to answer. In this story, God happened to answer the request the way Hezekiah wanted Him to.
3. When we pray, we need to trust God to do the best thing for us. Even though it may not be the answer we were wanting.
4. Make a sundial with your child.
5. First, press the clay or play-doh into the bottom of the flowerpot. Then push the chopstick into the clay. About three inches of the chopstick should stick up above the top of the flower pot.
6. In the morning, put your sundial outside in a sunny location. Make a mark on the rim of the pot where the stick's shadow lands. Write the time next to the mark.
7. Throughout the day, mark where the stick's shadow lands on the pot and record the time.
8. Leave the pot in the same spot and you will be able to use it to tell the approximate time of day by using the sun.

You Can Have a Relationship With God
You Need to Talk to God Regularly

Lesson Sixty-Five – Pour Our Your Heart

Materials: NIrV Bible – Jeremiah 29:11-13 and 2 Chronicles 7:14
Small Carpet Sample or Solid Welcome Mat
Various Colors of Permanent Markers or Paint

Preparation: Paint the words "My Prayer Mat" in the middle of the mat.

Lesson:
1. Ask your child if they can think of a way to communicate with someone who isn't in the same room with them. (i.e., letter, e-mail, phone, shouting, etc.)
2. Ask them if they have any idea how we can communicate with God. (pray)
3. Read the verses to your child.
4. Tell your child that God wants to be our best friend. He wants us to talk to Him about everything. He doesn't want us to be afraid or formal when we talk to Him.
5. Let your child create a prayer mat to kneel on when they pray. Have them decorate it by drawing or painting their handprints, flowers, designs, etc.
6. Once the mat dries, let your child place it beside their bed. It will help them remember to pray.

Lesson Sixty-Six – Jesus Prayed

Materials: None

Preparation: None

Story:

Today's story takes place early in the morning. The night before, Jesus had seen many, many people. He had spent time healing them and teaching them about God. Then He spent the night at Simon and Andrew's house. Can you imagine how much fun it would be to have Jesus spend the night at your house?

When it was early in the morning and still dark out, Jesus wanted to do something special. He walked outside quietly. He looked around for a place where He could be alone. Then He began to pray. Jesus wanted to start His day by talking to God. He knew that God would help Him get ready for the day.

Back at Simon and Andrew's house, everyone else started to wake up, too. Soon, they realized they didn't know where Jesus was. They called out, "Jesus! Jesus! Where are you?!?" Do you remember where He was? Yes, He was praying.

After searching for Jesus, they finally found Him. They ran up to Him and said, "We have been looking for you!" What do you think Jesus said? Jesus looked at them and said, "It's time to go to some new places. I need to tell more people about God's love. That is why I'm here on earth." So everyone gathered their things and followed Jesus. Many people heard Jesus and believed what He shared with them.

Jesus was showing us how important it is to spend time praying. Praying is talking with God. God loves it when we talk to Him. We can talk to Him anytime, anywhere. He will listen to you. You can tell Him anything you want.

Lesson:
1. Read the story to your child.
2. Spend some time playing hide and seek with your child. Take turns being Jesus (the one who is hiding.)

Lesson Sixty-Seven – Campfires and Burning Bushes

Materials: Candle

Preparation: None

Story:

      Today we are going to hear another story about Moses' life. When Moses was a grown-up, he did some naughty things in Egypt. He was afraid he would get in trouble, so we went to a different country. He thought he would be safe there.

      Life was hard for Moses. He had to learn how to be a shepherd. Remember, a shepherd takes care of sheep. Moses had grown up in Pharaoh's palace where he never had to do any work. Now that he was a shepherd, he had to learn how to work hard. He didn't have anyone helping him or giving him delicious food anymore.

      One day Moses was out in the fields with the sheep. As he was leading the sheep, they came to the mountain of God. Suddenly, Moses saw a strange thing. Moses saw fire coming out of a bush – but the bush was still green. Nothing was burning up or turning brown. Moses walked closer to get a better view.

      God saw that Moses was coming closer, so He called to him, "Moses, Moses!" Moses said, "I'm right here."

      Then God said, "Stay where you are. Take off your sandals because this is holy ground."

      Moses obeyed God and took off his sandals.

      God told Moses that He had seen Pharaoh treat His people badly. God had heard their cries for help. He told Moses that He had a plan. And Moses was part of the plan to get God's people out of Egypt. God told Moses to go and get His people.

      Moses just stood there. He was afraid. He didn't know what Pharaoh would say. He knew that there was a new Pharaoh now. The new Pharaoh didn't know Moses and he had heard that he was mean! So he told God that he wasn't a good leader. Moses wanted God to choose someone else.

      God asked Moses to throw down his shepherd's staff. It became a snake! Then he asked Moses to pick it up by the tail. It turned back into a staff. God explained that the people would see even more miracles and they would believe that God had sent Moses.

      Moses was still afraid. He told God he stuttered. That was no problem for God. God told him He would help him. He also told Moses that his brother, Aaron, could also help. So Moses took his family and traveled back to Egypt.

Lesson:
1. Read the story to your child.
2. Light a candle.
3. Have your child watch the flame and imagine how Moses must have felt when God talked to him out of the fire.

4. Discuss with your child how we don't need to wait to hear from God through a burning bush – we can talk to Him anytime. And God wants to hear from us every day.

Lesson Sixty-Eight – The Lord's Prayer

Materials: Latex Glove
                   Permanent Marker

Preparation: None

Story:

      Jesus' friends saw Him pray often. One time, after Jesus prayed, one of His friends asked Jesus to help them learn how to pray. Then Jesus taught them this simple prayer called The Lord's Prayer.
      First, tell God that you love Him. Praise Him for things that He has done.
      Second, ask God to help people to believe in Jesus.
      Third, ask God to help us with the things that we need for today.
      Fourth, ask God to forgive us for the naughty things that we have done.
      Fifth, ask God to help us to obey Him and to do the right thing.
      Jesus taught His friends a way that they can pray to God. We should remember that praying is talking to God. God wants us to talk to Him every day, all the time. He wants us to talk to Him like He is our best friend.

Lesson:
1. Read the story to your child.
2. Discuss with your child how Jesus taught His disciples how to pray – we should always start out by thanking God before we start asking for things.
3. Help your child to make a Prayer Glove. Write the following on each finger of the glove:
    a. Thumb = Father you are holy
    b. Pointer = Your kingdom will come
    c. 3rd finger = Give us the food we need
    d. Ring finger = Forgive us
    e. Pinky = Help us when we are tested
4. Practice saying the Lord's Prayer with your child every day for at least a week.

The Lord's Prayer
Our Father which art in heaven, Hallowed be Thy name.
Thy kingdom come. Thy will be done on earth, as it is in heaven.
Give us this day our daily bread.
And forgive us our debts, as we forgive our debtors.
And lead us not into temptation, but deliver us from evil:
For thine is the kingdom, and the power, and the glory, forever.
Amen.

Lesson Sixty-Nine – God Speaks to Samuel

Materials: None

Preparation: None

Story:

Long ago, there was a woman named Hannah who loved God. Hannah was sad because she didn't have any children. One day, Hannah prayed and asked God to give her a son. She promised that if He would, she would give him back to God when he got older.

God heard Hannah's prayer and He decided to bless her with a son. Hannah named her baby Samuel. When Samuel got older, Hannah kept her promise by sending Samuel to live at the church. He lived with a preacher named Eli.

Samuel helped Eli in the church. He was a good boy who loved God and always tried to obey Him. One night when Samuel was sleeping, he heard someone calling his name. He thought it was Eli. Samuel jumped up out of bed and ran to see what Eli wanted. Eli told him that he didn't call him.

Samuel went back to sleep. Again, he heard someone calling his name. He ran to see what Eli wanted. Eli told him that he hadn't called him.

Samuel went back to sleep. A third time, Samuel heard someone calling his name and went to Eli. Eli had not called. Suddenly, Eli realized that God was calling Samuel. Eli told Samuel to listen again for the voice. When he heard it, he must say, "I am here, God. I am listening."

Samuel lay back down. Sure enough, the voice called again and Samuel said, "I am here, God. I am listening."

God talked to Samuel and told him things that were going to happen. Samuel trusted God and listened to His voice. People everywhere came to know that Samuel loved God and that God spoke to people through Samuel.

Lesson:
1. Read the story to your child.
2. Have your child pretend that they are sleeping. Stand in the next room and whisper their name. Slowly step closer and whisper again until they can hear you.
3. After your child hears you, trade spots with them and let them try whispering your name.
4. Discuss with your child how sometimes God speaks out loud to people – but most of the time He speaks quietly to our heart.

Lesson Seventy – Jesus is Tempted

Materials: None

Preparation: None

Story:

It is important for us to read and learn verses from the Bible. Our story today talks about a time when Jesus was able to use Bible verses to fight off attacks from the devil.

One day, Jesus went out into the desert to pray. He stayed there a long time and He was very hungry. He had not eaten anything because He was trying to listen to God and do what He said.

The devil came to Jesus at this time. He knew Jesus would be weak with hunger and that this would be a good time to try to tempt Him to do something naughty. The devil came and told Jesus that He should turn a rock into bread so He would not be hungry. Jesus did not listen to the devil. Instead, Jesus said a Bible verse. He told the devil that it was more important to do what God says than what would make Jesus feel more comfortable.

Then, the devil took Jesus to the top of a church. He told Jesus that He should jump off. The devil said that if He jumped, an angel would catch Him and take care of Him. Again, Jesus did not listen to the devil. He said a Bible verse where God said that He didn't want people to test Him.

Then, the devil took Jesus to the top of a high mountain. He showed Jesus the entire world. The devil told Jesus He could have everything He saw if He would bow down to him. Jesus would not bow down to the devil. He told the devil to go away! He quoted another Bible verse which said that we are to only worship the One and True God and do what He says.

The devil tried three times to get Jesus to sin. But each time, Jesus did the right thing. He remembered Bible verses that helped Him to fight Satan.

Sometimes we may be tempted to do the wrong thing. God wants us to do good things! At these times, we need to remember Bible verses so we can fight the devil, just like Jesus did.

Lesson:
1. Read the story to your child.
2. Discuss how Jesus used the Bible to resist temptation.
3. Play "Make Me Laugh" with your child. Do and say silly things to try to make your child laugh. They need to try very hard not to laugh. (NOTE: You can't tickle or in any way touch your child – that would make it too hard for them to resist.)

4. After playing for awhile, ask your child if it was hard not to laugh when they really wanted to. Remind your child that it is difficult to resist temptation, but with God's help, we can do it.

Lesson Seventy-One – Sowing Seeds

Materials: Plastic Cups
                     Potting Soil
                     Sand
                     Gravel or Rocky Soil
                     Soil with a lot of Clay
                     Bean Seeds (or other fast-growing plant)

Preparation:

Story:

One day, Jesus told a story about some tiny seeds. A farmer was planting these seeds. The farmer would get a handful of seeds and carefully toss them onto the soil. Jesus said there were four different places where the tiny seeds could land.

The first place seeds landed was on the walking path. High up in the sky some birds saw those seeds. So the birds flew down and ate those seeds.

The second place seeds landed was by the rocks. Those seeds grew up quickly but they didn't have deep roots. When the sun came out and it became very hot, those poor little plants couldn't drink enough water with their weak roots. They all wilted.

The third place seeds landed was in the middle of some thorn bushes. These seeds started to grow, but the thorns choked the plants and they died.

The fourth place seeds landed was on good soil. They had plenty of water, fertilizer, and sunshine. They grew and made many vegetables.

Which seed would you like to be? The fourth set of seeds was happy because they were in a good place and they were growing. We can be happy and growing when we learn about Jesus by reading stories about Him and learning to obey Him. We will also be happy and growing when we go to church and when we pray.

Lesson:
1. Read the story to your child.
2. Discuss how the soil needs to be right for the seeds to grow. Talk about how the soil is our heart.
3. Show your child the different kinds of soil that you have gathered.
4. Have your child decide which kind of soil they think would be best for the seeds.
5. Fill the cups with the different soil. Help them plant a few seeds in each cup.
6. Water the seeds regularly and put them in a sunny location. Let your child observe which seeds grow better than others.

Lesson Seventy-Two – Hide Your Word in my Heart

Materials: NIrV Bible – Psalm 119:9-12
                         Long Balloons which can be twisted to make animal shapes

Preparation: None

Story:

These verses can be a little bit hard to understand. What does it mean to "hide God's word in your heart?" Well, I know that we call the Bible "The Word of God," but how could I hide it in my heart?!?

How do you hide something? To hide something, you put it somewhere so that it is out of sight. That means it is hidden from view.

If I take my Bible and lay it on the piano, is it hidden? No, of course it isn't. It is right there in plain sight. If I take my Bible and put it under my bed, is it hidden? Yes, it is. Now no one can see it.

Well, I understand what it means for something to be hidden, but how do you hide something in your heart? If I were to ask you to lie down on the floor, could I put the Bible on your chest and get it into your heart? No, that's silly, isn't it?

What if we went to a doctor? Could a doctor operate and put the Bible in our heart? I suppose he could, but I don't think it would be good for us to have a Bible in our heart.

If we can't put the Bible in our heart, then what does that verse mean? How does God's Word get into your heart? It gets there when we read and study the Bible every day until we will know it "by heart."

Did you know that we have to read, hear, or do something six times before it is in your head?!? So, for the Bible to get from our head to our heart, we need to read the Bible every day.

Lesson:
1. Read the Bible verses to your child.
2. Read the story to your child.
3. Tell you child that while we are hiding God's word in our hearts, He is shaping us into the kind of person He wants us to be.
4. Blow up the balloons and form them into different animal shapes for your child.

Lesson Seventy-Three – The Sword of the Spirit

Materials: Pictures of Armor (see companion download)
              Cardboard (Old boxes, whatever you can find)
              Duct Tape or Masking Tape
              Aluminum Foil
              Crayons or Markers
              Scissors
              Yarn

Preparation: Print the pictures of armor from the companion download.

Story: (show your child the armor pictures which are highlighted while telling them the story)

Did you know that as Christians we are in God's army? And that God calls the Bible a sword?!? He certainly does. God gave us some mighty weapons to help protect us from the devil's mean ways and to help us stand up for Jesus.

God said that we need to have the **Belt of Truth** buckled around our waist. God's truth will hold us up just like a belt holds up our pants.

Next, we need the **Breastplate of Righteousness**. A breastplate is a piece of metal which protects a soldier from the neck to the waist. Most importantly, it covers the heart. God wants us to live right lives. When we do this, we are protecting our heart.

We also need to have **Peaceful Feet** which are ready for action. We need to be at peace with God and ready to go tell others about how they can find God's peace by believing in Jesus.

God said that we also need the **Shield of Faith**. A shield is used to protect the soldier from fiery arrows. In the same way, our trust in Jesus will help us when Satan tries to shoot arrows at us. These arrows are things like mean thoughts, lies, and gossip. Instead of thinking mean thoughts, we stop these arrows with our shield and live like Jesus.

A soldier also needs to protect his head. God said we would need our **Helmet of Salvation**. We need to think about God so the devil can't put little lies in our mind that draw us away from Him. Salvation means that Jesus made a way to save us. Jesus died on the cross for all the naughty things that we have done. He took our punishment for us. We must believe in Him and tell Him that we are sorry for all the wrong things that we have done. We must also ask Him to be the Lord of our lives. Then He will make us clean and help us to follow Him.

The last piece of equipment we need is the **Sword of the Spirit**. Our sword is the Bible. The more verses we learn and memorize in our hearts, the more we are protected from doing wrong things. Just like a soldier has to get his instructions from a leader, we need to get our directions from God.

Lesson:
1. Read the story to your child.
2. Discuss with your child how important it is to read the Bible so that God can give us His instructions for our lives.
3. Using the materials for this lesson, make armor with your child. You can make a shield, a sword, a helmet… the possibilities are limitless. Let your child decorate it and wear it. They will love using their imagination!
4. NOTE: You will probably have to cut the cardboard pieces out because it's so thick. Let your child tell you how to cut, though, so that the armor can be his creation.

You Can Be All God Wants You to Be
God Wants You to be Good, Kind, and Loving Just like Him

Lesson Seventy-Four – I Forgive You

Materials: Glass Jar with a Narrow Opening
Candy

Preparation: Put the candy in the jar. The jar opening should be big enough for them to reach through, but should not be able to get their hand out if they are gripping any candy.

Story:

      Our story today is about a man named Joseph. Joseph's father loved him very much and had a special coat made for him. His brothers were jealous and sold him into slavery. Joseph ended up in prison in Egypt for something he didn't even do. But God was with Joseph and helped him through the hard times that he had.

      One day, the Pharaoh had a dream that bothered him. He sent for Joseph to help him understand his dream. God told Joseph that they would have seven good years with plenty of food and then seven hard years with not enough food. Pharaoh asked Joseph to be in charge. He gave him a special ring and a robe, too.

      During the seven good years, Joseph made sure that they saved plenty of food. He organized everything in such a way that the land of Egypt would have plenty during the hard years that were coming.

      During the hard times, Joseph's father and brothers didn't have enough food to eat. Joseph's father told his other sons to go to Egypt to get food for the family. They had to travel a long way to get to Egypt.

      When they finally got there, they were sent to see Joseph. Joseph realized who they were, but they did not recognize that he was their brother. Joseph decided to see if they had changed their ways. Years before, they had really hurt Joseph. He wondered if they were sorry for the wrong things that they had done.

      Joseph tested his brothers and found that they had changed. They were sorry for the naughty things they had done to him in the past. Joseph was so excited that he told them who he was. The brothers were silent. They were afraid that Joseph would hurt them because of what they had done to him years before. Instead, Joseph told them that he had forgiven them and that God had been with him the whole time.

      Joseph gathered the whole family and let them stay with him in Egypt. They had plenty to eat and God watched over them all. God was pleased with Joseph. He also wants us to forgive others and to love them like He loves us.

Lesson:
1. Read the story to your child.
2. Discuss with your child how Joseph forgave his brothers even though they had been mean to him.

3. Have your child reach into the jar and try to pull out some candy. Their hand should be stuck. They will have to drop the candy before they can remove their hand.
4. Explain to your child that we need to drop or let go of the bad feelings we have when people hurt us in order to forgive them. Talk about how God wants us to forgive people. Explain that God promises to take care of things and it is not up to us to try to make things right or take revenge when others hurt us.
5. Let your child enjoy some of the candy.

Lesson Seventy-Five – Have the Right Attitude

Materials: Paper
                Markers or Crayons

Preparation: None

Story:

While Jesus was on earth, many people loved to sit and listen to Him talk about God and how much He loved them. One day Jesus shared some special news with His friends. He told them how to be happy and to have good attitudes. The people listened and learned many things. Jesus told them that they would be happy if they kept learning more and more about God. He told them that God loved them very much and He cared about all of their needs. Jesus told them to help others and to always try to do the right thing.

Jesus told the people that helping others would make them really happy. The people smiled and went home trying to follow God and help others.

God wants us to have good attitudes and to be happy, too. Let's ask God to help us love Him and to love others. Let's ask Him to help us to always have the right attitude.

Lesson:
1. Read the story to your child.
2. Have your child draw a picture of three things for which they are thankful.
3. Discuss with your child how everything good that we have is a gift from God – and we need to be thankful for it.

Lesson Seventy-Six – Helping Others

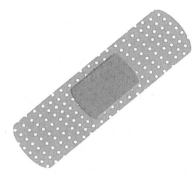

Materials: Stuffed Animal
                Ace wrap or gauze

Preparation: None

Story:

    Jesus loved to tell stories to people to help them know how they should act. One day Jesus told them a story about how we should be helpful to people. Here's the story:

    A Jewish man was traveling on a dangerous road one day. As he went along, he was attacked by robbers. They took his clothes, beat him, and robbed him. The poor man was left for dead on the side of the road.

    A priest happened to be traveling on that same road. When he saw the hurt man, he thought about the good things he would be late for if he stopped to help the man. He crossed to the other side of the road and kept on walking.

    A Levite also saw the hurt man and passed him by.

    Then a Samaritan man came along. Samaritans and Jews were enemies. But when he saw the hurt man he had pity on him. He went to him and bandaged his wounds. Then he put him on his donkey and took him to an inn. The next day he took out some money and gave it to the innkeeper. "Look after him," the Samaritan man said, "and when I return, I will pay you back for any extra expense you may have."

    Jesus told this story so we would see how we should treat people. We shouldn't be so concerned about the things we are planning to do that we don't have time to help people when they need it.

Lesson:
1. Read the story to your child.
2. Have your child pretend that one of their stuffed animals is hurt.
3. Have your child practice being a Good Samaritan to it.
4. Remind your child that God wants us to be helpful to everyone, whether they're our friends or our enemies.

Lesson Seventy-Seven – I'm Sorry

Materials: Green Construction Paper
               Yellow Construction Paper
               Tape
               Crayons or Markers

Preparation: None

Story:

Jesus told another story to help people understand how we need to forgive people. Here is the story:

Once upon a time, there was a king who wanted to get all his money matters in order. One man who owed him lots of money was brought in to see him. The man did not have any money to pay his debt.

The man fell to his knees. He begged the king to have patience with him. Surprisingly, the king looked at the man and told him that he did not have to pay him back. The man was so excited that he had been forgiven. He could not believe it!

After the man left the king, he ran into a servant who owed him a few dollars. He grabbed the servant by his throat and began to choke him. He demanded that the servant pay him back.

The servant fell to the ground, just as the man had done with the king, and begged for help.

"Please, sir, be patient with me!"

Do you know what that man did? He had the servant thrown into jail. He did not forgive him.

Several other men saw what had happened. They knew that the man had been treated kindly by the king. They also saw how the man showed no mercy or forgiveness to the servant who owed him very little. It was as if he had forgotten how kind the king had been toward him.

The men ran to the king and told him what had happened.

The king called the man to come to him. "You naughty man," he said. "I forgave your debt because you begged me. Shouldn't you do the same with the man who begged you?" The king was so angry that he threw the man into jail until he could pay back everything he owed.

Jesus told this story so we can remember how we must also show forgiveness and love toward others – even when they have done wrong to us. We must remember all of the naughty things we have done for which God has given us forgiveness. That will remind us to forgive others when they do something wrong to us.

Lesson:
1. Read the story to your child.
2. Remind your child that God wants us to be good and kind to others. When we do something that isn't kind, we need to ask people for forgiveness.
3. Make paper money and crowns. Act out the story with your child.

Lesson Seventy-Eight – Thank You

Materials: None

Preparation: None

Story:

  Jesus was traveling to Jerusalem. On His way, He was met by ten men who had leprosy. When people had this disease they had to stay outside of town and loudly call out "unclean" whenever anyone walked by. They could never touch anyone for fear that they would give the disease to someone else.
  When these men saw Jesus, they stood at a distance from Him and called out, "Jesus, Master, have pity on us!"
  When Jesus saw the men He told them to go show themselves to their priest. As they were walking away, they were healed of their disease.
  When one of the men noticed that he was healed, he came back to Jesus and praised God in a loud voice. He threw himself at Jesus' feet and thanked Him.
  Jesus asked, "Didn't I heal ten men? Where are the other nine? Are you the only one who is going to return and give thanks and praise to God?" Then Jesus said to the man, "Get up and go home. Your faith has made you well."
  Jesus was disappointed that He healed ten men but only one of the men came back and said thank you. The Bible says that "every good and perfect gift is from above, and comes down from the Father of lights" (James 1:17.) This means that everything good that happens in our life is a gift from God. We need to make sure we give thanks to God every time something good happens to us.

Lesson:
1. Read the story to your child.
2. Have your child jump up and down ten times.
3. Each time they jump, have them say, "Thank-you, Jesus!"
4. Remind your child that God wants us to be thankful to Him.

Lesson Seventy-Nine – Jesus Changes Saul

Materials: Water
                      Clear Cups
                      Food Coloring

Preparation: None

Story:

      Saul was a man who did not believe that Jesus was the Son of God. In fact, he was so mad at the people who did believe in Jesus that he would help arrest them and have them killed.

      One day, as Saul was traveling to a town, something strange happened. A bright light from Heaven suddenly flashed around him. Saul fell to the ground. He heard a voice saying to him, "Saul, Saul! Why are you doing things to hurt Me?!?"

      Saul said, "Who are you, Lord?"

      The voice answered, "I am Jesus. I am the One you are trying to hurt. Get up, now, and go into the city. Someone there will tell you what you must do."

      Saul got up from the ground. He opened his eyes – but he could not see! So, the men who were with Saul had to lead him to the city. For three days, Saul did not eat or drink anything.

      In the city, there was a man named Ananias. He loved Jesus very much. The Lord spoke to him and said, "Get up and go to the street called Straight Street. Find the house of Judas. Ask for a man named Saul from the city of Tarsus. He is praying in the house.

      Ananias was afraid. He answered, "Lord, many people have told me about this man. He has done terrible things to people who believe in You."

      The Lord said to Ananias, "Go! I have chosen Saul for some important work. He believes in Me now and he will tell many people about Me.

      So Ananias obeyed God. He went to the house God told him about and found Saul. He put his hands on Saul's eyes and something like fish scales fell off. Immediately Saul could see! But there was a difference in what he now saw. He not only could see physically again, but now he saw everything with new eyes – spiritually. Before, Saul wanted to hurt Jesus' friends and even kill them. But now he loved Jesus and wanted to serve Him.

      Saul got up and was baptized because he wanted everyone to know that he believed in Jesus. Saul's name was later changed to Paul to show the change in his heart. Paul stayed in town and told people about Jesus' love. He shared with them how Jesus had changed his life. He told them how much God loved them.

      All the people were amazed. They knew that Jesus had definitely changed his life.

Lesson:
1. Read the story to your child.
2. Ask your child what Saul did when he was bad.
3. Ask your child what Paul did when he was good.
4. Ask your child who it is that changed Paul and helped him to be good.
5. Show your child the clear glass of water. Put a drop of food coloring into the cup. Let your child see how the water changes colors.
6. Share how Jesus changes us on the inside when we believe in Him. Tell your child that when they feel like they want to do something bad, they need to pray and ask God to help them to be good.
7. Go through different real-life scenarios with your child that they might face. Work through what they should do in each situation.

Lesson Eighty – Bad Choices

Materials: Paper
               Red Tissue Paper
               Glue
               Crayons or Markers
               An Apple

Preparation: Draw a tree on the paper. Try to include several bare branches at the top of the tree.

Story:

   Adam was the first person in the world. God had created Adam and He loved him very much. God let Adam be in charge of naming all the animals. Name some animals that you know.
   God saw that Adam needed someone like him to be his friend. So God created a woman and He named her Eve. God made a beautiful garden for Adam and Eve to live in. There were beautiful flowers and animals everywhere. They could eat any fruit from any tree, except for one special tree. God told them that they were not allowed to eat the fruit from that tree or they would die.
   One day a snake hissed at Eve. He was trying to trick Eve. The snake told Eve that she should eat the fruit from the special tree because then she would be smart like God.
   Eve looked at the fruit. She picked it and ate it. It did taste good! Then she gave some of the fruit to Adam. Adam also ate the fruit.
   Suddenly, they knew that God was near and they were scared. They hid in the bushes because they knew that they had disobeyed God.
   God called for them and asked them why they were in the bushes. He knew why, but He wanted them to tell Him. Adam and Eve told God what they had done.
   God was sad that they had disobeyed Him. He still loved them but He knew that He had to punish them for disobeying Him.
   God told them they had to leave the beautiful garden. He told them that He would still take care of them; but, life would be a lot harder because they had chosen to disobey. Also, they would die someday as a punishment for their sin.
   Adam and Eve still loved God. They had to learn a hard lesson because of their mistake. They tried hard to listen and obey God after that.
   We need to listen and obey God, too. We must also listen to and obey our parents. It's not always easy to obey; but, we can pray and ask God to help us when we are having trouble doing the right thing.

Lesson:
1. Read the story to your child.
2. Discuss with your child how Adam and Eve made a bad choice. Present different scenarios to your child such as sharing/not sharing, obeying/disobeying, etc. and ask them which would be the good choice and which would be the bad choice.
3. Have your child tear pieces of red tissue paper off and crumple them into balls.
4. Help your child to glue these balls to the tree branches.
5. Share an apple with your child as you work.

Lesson Eighty-One – Abel Obeys

Materials: Stepping Stool
                   Some Vegetables

Preparation: Fill a sink with water. Put the stepping stool up to the sink so your child can actively participate.

Story:

At the time of today's story, Adam and Eve had two children. Cain was the first son and Abel was the second son. Cain was a farmer. He worked in the garden. Can you think of some vegetables he must have planted?

Abel was a shepherd. He took care of the sheep. What kind of sound does a sheep make?

Cain and Abel knew that when they did something naughty, they would have to bring an animal to use as a blood sacrifice to give to God. God told them exactly what kind of gift to bring in order to receive His forgiveness for their sins.

One day, both brothers made a sacrifice to God. Cain brought some of his vegetables to God as a gift. Abel brought the best part of his best sheep as a gift to God. He gave his best to God. He also obeyed God by bringing the kind of sacrifice that God had asked for.

God looked down and was happy with Abel's obedience. But God was not happy with Cain's disobedience. So Cain got angry and he began to frown.

God said to Cain, "Why are you angry? Why are you frowning? You can do what is right. Please don't do wrong."

Do you know what Cain did? He could have listened to God and brought the right kind of sacrifice... but he didn't. Instead, he felt jealousy toward his brother, Abel. In his anger, Cain decided to kill Abel.

Because of Cain's sin, God had to punish Cain even more.

God wants us to always obey Him and do what is right. He loves us and wants to help us.

Lesson:
1. Read the story to your child.
2. Discuss with your child how God wants us to obey Him and to obey our parents.
3. Talk about how Cain was punished because he tried to do things his way instead of God's way. Talk with your child about how things might have been different if he had listened to God.
4. Let your child help wash some vegetables to help them remind them of Cain's improper sacrifice.

Lesson Eighty-Two – Making Peace

Materials: Paper
                Crayons or Markers

Preparation: None

Story:

      Abraham's son, Isaac, grew up and married a woman named Rebekah. When it came time, Rebekah had twin boys. Do you know what twins are? They are two babies who are born at the same time. Sometimes they look alike, but not always. These babies looked different. The first baby was reddish in color. He was hairy, too. They named him Esau.

      The second baby was holding onto Esau's foot when he was born. They named him Jacob, which means "grabber." Esau loved to hunt and work outside in the fields. Jacob liked to stay inside the tents and cook.

      One day, Esau came into the tent. He was starving! His tummy was rumbling. Jacob was cooking a delicious vegetable soup. It smelled so good! Jacob decided to do something sneaky. He told Esau that he could have some soup if he would give Jacob a special gift that their father was planning to give Esau. Esau was so hungry that he agreed to give Jacob his special gift!

      Later on, Esau was angry at how Jacob had tricked him. Jacob knew that he was in trouble, so he went to live with their uncle for a long time.

      Years passed without Jacob seeing Esau. During that time, Jacob changed his ways. He stopped being tricky and started following God.

      One day, it came time for the brothers to meet. Jacob was nervous about it. He wasn't sure what his brother would do. When Esau saw Jacob, he rushed to him and hugged him. He forgave Jacob for everything wrong that he had done to him.

      God wants us to forgive others like Esau forgave Jacob.

Lesson:
1. Read the story to your child.
2. Talk to your child about someone your child sometimes has trouble getting along with, such as a brother, a sister, or a friend. Discuss with your child how we need to try to get along with everyone – and God will help us if we ask Him.
3. Help your child to make a card for that person. If your child has been fighting with this person, write "I'm sorry" on the card for them.
4. Help your child to deliver this card to the person and to apologize if necessary.

Lesson Eighty-Three – Four Good Friends

Materials: Blanket
               Stuffed Animal

Preparation: None

Story:

    One day Jesus was teaching inside a house. People came from all around to listen to Jesus and to see the miracles He did. In fact, so many people came that the house was full!

    Four friends heard where Jesus was. They had a friend who was sick and couldn't walk. They decided to carry their friend to the house where Jesus was. When they got to the house, however, there were so many people that they could not find a way to get to Jesus!

    One of the friends had an idea. In those days, some houses had stairs on the outside. The men climbed up the stairs carrying their friend with them. The roof of the house was made of tree branches and straw. Once they made it to the roof, they pulled the straw and branches apart enough to make a hole right above where Jesus was teaching. Can you imagine what the people inside the house must have thought?!?

    The friends lowered the man down right in front of Jesus. What a surprise! Jesus saw that the men believed in Him and how much they loved their friend. Instead of making the man well, however, He said, "Friend, your sins are forgiven."

    Some of the teachers heard what Jesus said and they were upset. They didn't understand how Jesus could say this since only God can forgive sins. They did not know that Jesus was God's Son.

    Jesus knew what they were thinking. He looked at the man who couldn't walk and He said, "Get up, take your mat, and go home."

    Immediately, the man stood up in front of them, took what he had been lying on, and went home thanking God. Everyone was amazed and thanked God.

    Jesus loves it when we do our best to help our friends. We should always do whatever we can to help others.

Lesson:
1. Read the story to your child.
2. Discuss how the friends were willing to try to help their friend when he needed help. Talk about how we also need to be willing to help others.
3. Put the stuffed animal on the blanket.
4. Have your child hold two corners of the blanket and you hold the other two.
5. Carry the blanket around the house pretending you are taking the stuffed animal to see Jesus.

Lesson Eighty-Four – Loyalty

Materials: None

Preparation: None

Story:

     A woman named Naomi and her husband lived in the town of Bethlehem. They had two sons. There was not enough food to eat where they lived so they moved their family to the land of Moab. One of Naomi's sons married a woman named Ruth.

     Years later, Naomi's husband died. Then her sons died. Naomi decided to go back to her hometown. Ruth told Naomi that she wanted to stay with her. Ruth left everything to follow Naomi.

     Ruth and Naomi traveled to Bethlehem. When they arrived, the people in the town became excited. The people were so glad to see Naomi and her daughter-in-law, Ruth.

     One day, Naomi told Ruth to the fields to collect the leftover grain so they would be able to make bread to eat. Ruth went to Boaz's field. She didn't know that he was part of Naomi's family. Ruth patiently gathered grain. Later, Boaz saw her and told his workers to give her lots of grain. He spoke to Ruth and told her not to go anywhere else – that he would help her and Naomi with all of their needs. He liked Ruth.

     When Naomi saw how much grain Ruth brought home, she was excited! She knew that God was looking out for them. Naomi had a plan. She told Ruth to dress up and quietly sit down by Boaz after he had eaten supper and was asleep. Ruth did all that Naomi asked. Sure enough, Boaz woke up and found Ruth at his feet. He told her that he would marry her.

     Boaz was so happy. He told the group that he would marry Ruth. Later, Ruth and Boaz had a son. They named him Obed. God took care of Naomi and Ruth. They loved God and He made sure that they were cared for.

     God was very pleased that Ruth was so loyal to Naomi. Ruth put her own needs aside to look out for her mother-in-law and God rewarded her in the end by bringing her a happy marriage to Boaz.

Lesson:
1. Read the story to your child.
2. Talk about how Ruth was loyal to Naomi and followed her even when it meant she would have to move to a strange place.
3. Play "Follow the Leader" with your child.

Lesson Eighty-Five – Friendship

Materials: Two Pennies
                      String
                      Two Pieces of Paper
                      Glue
                      Yarn
                      Crayons

Preparation:
1. Glue the pennies onto the paper as eyes.
2. Glue the yarn onto the paper to form a head, nose, and smile.
3. Let the face dry before doing this lesson with your child.

Story:

David was a man who loved God. His best friend was Jonathan. Jonathan was the son of King Saul. They were wonderful friends and did many things together.

King Saul was jealous of David because God helped David to do many great things. Saul tried several times to kill David. He wanted his son, Jonathan, to be the next king instead of David.

Jonathan loved David. He knew that God had decided that David would be the next king. He was happy for his best friend.

One day, David talked to Jonathan about King Saul. David was scared of the king and had been hiding in the fields. David wanted to know if he was safe or in danger. Jonathan told David that he would always be his friend and he would promise to take care of his family if something ever happened to him.

There was a banquet the next day at the king's house. David told Jonathan that if he did not show up for the banquet and the king became angry, he would know that he was in great danger. Jonathan told David that he would shoot an arrow in the field as a secret sign to let him know if he was safe or in danger.

Sure enough, that night at the banquet, King Saul asked about David. Jonathan told him that he was not coming and King Saul was furious! Saul yelled at Jonathan. Jonathan knew that David was in danger.

The next day, Jonathan shot the arrow in the field giving the secret sign to let David know that he was in danger. David and Jonathan were sad. They knew that they would never see each other again. They again promised to care for each other's families and to be friends forever.

God wants us to be friends like Jonathan and David. He wants us to love others and put their needs before our own.

Lesson:
1. Read the story to your child.
2. Discuss how Jonathan was a friend to David and God wants us to be friends to others.
3. Show your child the friendly face that you created earlier.
4. Place a piece of paper over the face and help your child to do a rubbing with the side of a crayon. The outline and textures of the face will appear on the top paper.

Lesson Eighty-Six – Courage

Materials: Empty Paper Towel Roll
Aluminum Foil
Markers
Beads and Fake Jewels (optional)
Glue

Preparation: None

Story:

Long ago, there was a woman named Esther. God had helped her to become the queen. She was a beautiful woman who loved God very much. Her adopted father was named Mordecai. He cared for her and made sure she was safe.

One day, Mordecai was upset. Esther sent someone to find out what was wrong. Mordecai told her some sad news. The king had made a bad law that all of God's people should be killed. He knew that a mean man had tricked the king into making this law. The king didn't even know that Esther was one of God's people!

Mordecai asked Esther to help. He told her that God had put her there as queen to help God's people. Esther was afraid and scared. She knew that she could only go to the king if he invited her. If she went uninvited, the king had to hold out his royal scepter to give her permission to enter. If he didn't, then Esther would be killed. She asked her people to pray to God for her. They prayed for three days.

On the third day, Esther put on her royal robes. Then she took a deep breath and walked into the inner room where the king was seated. The king saw Esther and he was pleased. He held out his royal scepter and invited her into his room! Then the king asked Esther what she wanted. Instead of telling him the news, she invited the king and the mean man to come the next day for a banquet.

The next day, as they were eating, the king asked Esther what she wanted. Esther asked the king to let her live. She also asked him to let her people live. She explained that all of her people were going to be killed.

The king couldn't believe this. He wanted to know who planned to kill them.

Esther spoke up and told him the mean man had planned the whole thing. She pleaded with the king for her people's lives. The king made a command that all of God's people could gather and fight anyone who tried to kill them.

God was with His people. They were victorious. Afterwards, they had a special feast to honor God for saving His people. Esther had courage. She was brave to approach the king, even though she knew she might be killed for doing it. God wants us to trust Him as Esther did and to be courageous, always trying to do the right thing.

Lesson:
1. Read the story to your child.
2. Discuss how the king would have to extend his royal scepter to let Esther talk. If he hadn't done so, she would have been killed for approaching the king without his permission.
3. Tell your child that Esther was courageous to approach the king. Talk about how God will give us courage to do the right thing as well if we ask for His help.
4. Help your child to make a royal scepter. Glue sheets of aluminum foil to the outside of the paper towel roll.
5. Let your child decorate the outside of their scepter.

Lesson Eighty-Seven – Patience

Materials: Big Bowl
Treat that your child somewhat enjoys
Treat that your child LOVES

Preparation: None

Story:

Hannah and her husband lived in Ramah. They loved God and went to church. Hannah's husband loved her. But Hannah was sad. She did not have any children. People would laugh at Hannah because she didn't have any kids. Hannah cried and cried.

One day, Hannah decided to go to church and pray. She prayed very hard! She promised God that if He gave her a son, she would dedicate him to God. She would let him stay with the priest and learn about God and the church.

The priest's name was Eli. He saw her praying and went up to her. Hannah told Eli what she was praying for. Eli told her that he was sure God would answer her prayers.

Sure enough, Hannah did have a child. It was a boy! She named him Samuel which means "I asked the Lord for him." She rocked her baby every day. She taught Samuel about God. She was glad that God had given her this son. She remembered that she must keep her promise to God.

When Samuel was old enough, Hannah took him to church. She let Eli take care of him and teach him even more about God. Each year, Hannah visited Samuel and brought him a new coat. She loved Samuel and was so grateful to God that He had answered her prayers.

God wants us to be patient as Hannah was patient. When we are having a hard time waiting for something, we need to talk to God about it just as Hannah did.

Lesson:
1. Put a treat your child somewhat enjoys into the bowl. Show it to your child. When they want to take the treat, tell them that they need to be patient and wait until later – that it will be better if they wait.
2. Read the story to your child.
3. If your child waits patiently, then exchange the treat they somewhat enjoy for the treat that they LOVE and let them take it from the bowl.
4. As your child enjoys his treat, explain to him that God can always be trusted to give us His best if we are patient and wait for the right time.

Lesson Eighty-Eight – Don't Complain

Materials: 1 cup Lemon Juice (about 4 lemons)
                    3 cups Cold Water
                    ½ cup Sugar (amount varies according to your preferences)

Preparation: None

Story:

Have you ever heard someone complain about something? You may have heard someone say, "I don't like that!" or "This tastes yucky!" or "I don't want to do that!" Maybe you've even said those things yourself.

If doesn't feel good to hear someone complain. It hurts people and makes them start seeing things in a bad way instead of a good way. The people in our story had a problem with complaining and learned a hard lesson from it.

Moses had a brother named Aaron and a sister named Miriam. They loved their brother and traveled with him when God led the people out of Egypt.

God led His people through the hot, hot desert. God gave the people everything they needed. He gave them food and water. God even made sure that their clothes and shoes didn't wear out as they were walking!

When things got hard, however, the people would start to complain. Aaron and Miriam started to complain as well. They complained about living in the desert, about eating manna, and even about Moses' wife!

God heard their complaining and wanted to teach them a lesson. God asked Moses, Aaron and Miriam to step outside the church tent. Then He asked Aaron and Miriam to step forward. God came down in the form of a cloud and told them that He did not like their complaining attitudes. When the cloud was gone, Miriam was covered with a white sickness.

Aaron turned to Moses and told him that he was sorry for complaining. Then he asked Moses to help them.

Moses called out to God and asked Him to heal Miriam. God told Moses that she would have to sit outside the camp for seven days. After that, she would be healed. Miriam had a whole week to tell God she was sorry. She also saw that complaining and grumbling only hurts people including ourselves.

God wants us to say kind things to others. Instead of telling someone that we do not like something, He wants us to either keep quiet or find something else nice to say instead.

Lesson:
1. Read the story to your child.
2. Mix up the lemonade but leave out the sugar. It will be very bitter and sour.
3. Let your child take a tiny sip of this lemonade.
4. Discuss with your child how complaining makes a person very bitter and sour, like the lemonade.
5. Now add the sugar to the lemonade and let your child take a nice, big drink.

6. Explain to your child how sweetness and kindness help others and encourage them.
7. Ask your child how they can try to be "sugar" for others this week.

Lesson Eighty-Nine – The Golden Rule

Materials: None

Preparation: **You will be taking a trip to a fast food restaurant for this lesson** – or you can improvise by doing something similar at home.

Story:

     One day Jesus was talking to people when one man asked Him a good question. He asked Jesus what God's most important rule was.

     Jesus told the man the most important rule was to love God with all of our heart. Then Jesus told the man there was another important rule to obey. Jesus told him we must love other people as we love ourselves.

     Jesus wants us to know that we should love God the most, love others second, and love ourselves last. How can we show that we love God? How can we show that we love other people?

Lesson:
1. Read the story to your child.
2. Go inside a fast food restaurant and get napkins, condiments, etc. Then sit down with your child.
3. Pass out the items to your child and tell them to enjoy their hamburger.
4. When your child protests that they don't have a hamburger say, "Oops! I forgot to get the most important thing – the hamburger!"
5. Discuss with your child how God also wants us to remember the most important thing – to love God and to love other people. He doesn't want us to forget it.
6. Now go buy a hamburger for you and your child and enjoy.

You Can Be All God Wants You to Be
God Wants You to be See and Think Good Things

Lesson Ninety – I Need to Follow the Rules

Materials: ½ cup Brown Sugar
                   ½ cup Peanut Butter
                   1 Tbsp. Granola
                   Toothpick

Preparation: None

Story:

     We have been hearing many stories about God's people. Moses was God's friend. He helped the people to follow God.

     One day while they were in the hot desert, God told Moses to climb up a special mountain. Moses climbed and climbed up the mountain. When he got to the top, he saw lots of smoke. God spoke to Moses through the smoke clouds.

     God told Moses ten important rules the people should follow. These rules were called commandments. The first four commandments taught the people to love God more than anything else. They also told the people not to use God's name in a bad way. They helped people to see how important it was to go to church and to worship God.

     The next six commandments taught the people how to love others. God told us to obey our parents, to tell the truth, to be honest, not to steal, and not to wish for things that other people have.

     God wrote these rules down on two stone tablets to help the people remember them. All of these rules are important because they help us remember to love God and to love others.

Lesson:
1. Read the story to your child.
2. Discuss how God gave us rules to keep us safe – and we need to obey those rules.
3. Mix the brown sugar, the peanut butter and the granola.
4. Shape the ingredients into tablets.
5. Write a commandment on the tablet using a toothpick.
6. Eat your edible commandments.

Lesson Ninety-One – Strong Samson

Materials: Construction Paper
                      Scissors

Preparation: None

Story:

Long ago, a baby boy named Samson was born. God told his parents that this would be a special boy who would be dedicated to His service. The parents were never to cut this little boy's hair.

Samson grew to be a very strong man. In fact, he was the strongest man in the world. Unfortunately, Samson didn't always use his God-given strength to make God look good. He usually wanted to make himself look good.

Samson would tell silly riddles to try to make himself look good. He didn't do things that he knew he should do. And Samson's spent a lot of time hanging around people who did not love God. Isn't that sad?!? Samson was about to learn a very hard lesson about having to be punished when he didn't obey.

This lesson started when Samson fell in love with a woman named Delilah. Delilah did not love God. Even worse, Delilah's people were God's enemies, the Philistines. Samson parents had already warned him that he shouldn't be spending time with this kind of woman. But Samson didn't listen to his parents.

The leaders of the Philistines saw that Samson was spending a lot of time with Delilah. They wanted to hurt Samson; but they couldn't because he was so strong. So, they asked Delilah if she would find out the secret of what made Samson so strong.

Delilah agreed. She asked Samson, "What makes you so strong? How can you be tied up and taken captive?"

Now this is a strange question to ask someone. Maybe Samson was suspicious because he didn't tell Delilah the truth at first. He lied to Delilah several times, telling her things that wouldn't take away his strength. Delilah kept trying to tie him up as Samson told her to do. Then the Philistines would burst into the room and Samson would break free easily.

This happened several times. Finally, after Delilah nagged him about his secret for days and days, Samson grew so tired of her questions that he decided to tell her the truth. He told her that if his hair was shaved off, then he would become as weak as any other man. Samson never should have told her this because he had made a vow with God to never have his hair cut!

When Samson went to sleep that night, Delilah shaved Samson's hair from his head. This broke his vow to God and Samson's amazing strength left him. When the Philistines burst into his room this time, they were able to capture Samson easily.

God had given Samson a special gift – amazing strength – and Samson wasted that strength in doing things that didn't make God or his parents happy. Fortunately, God gave Samson another chance to make things right at the end of his life.

Lesson:
1. Read the story to your child.
2. Discuss how God gave Samson great strength – but Samson didn't use that strength to bring glory to God. Talk about how we need to use the talents that God gives to us in a way that would make Him happy.
3. Help your child cut the construction paper into a headband and strips for a wig.
4. Have them pretend to be Samson and you can be Delilah. Let them wear the wig and you can come in and cut his paper "hair" off.

Lesson Ninety-Two – Busy, Busy, Busy

Materials: Paper Grocery Sack
                Scissors
                Crayons or Markers

Preparation: None

Story:

Our story today is about two sisters in the Bible. They were friends of Jesus. One day they heard that He was coming to visit them and they were very excited.

One of the sisters, Martha, loved to cook. She began to think of all the special things she would like to cook for Jesus. What would you like to cook for Jesus if He were coming to our house for dinner?

Mary was the other sister. She was excited because she wanted to hear all the things Jesus had to say and learn about all the places He had been.

Mary watched out the window for Jesus to come. Suddenly she saw Him. She was so excited that she ran out to see Him. Martha stayed and finished her cooking.

Other friends came to see Jesus, too. They all sat down to eat the delicious meal that Martha had made. Mary sat down, too. She wanted to hear every word that Jesus said. She had forgotten about the food. She wanted to listen to Jesus.

Martha was in the kitchen by herself. She was getting tired and upset. She was mad because Mary was not helping. She was only sitting down and listening. Martha got so angry that she went straight to Jesus and asked Him to make Mary help her.

Jesus told Martha that she should not worry about what others do. He told her that Mary was doing something important. She was listening to Him and learning. Martha was not wrong because she was cooking. She was wrong because she was not putting Jesus first. Jesus helped her to see that she should do what Jesus wants her to do and let Him take care of what others are doing.

Jesus wants us to listen and learn about Jesus just like Mary listened to Jesus.

Lesson:
1. Read the story to your child.
2. Discuss how we should never get so busy that we don't have time to spend with God praying and reading the Bible.
3. Let your child decorate their grocery sack to look like an apron.

4. Help them to cut a hole in the top for their head and two holes in the sides for their arms.

Lesson Ninety-Three – We Need to Believe

Materials: Timer

Preparation: None

Story:

During the time of King Herod, there was a priest name Zechariah. His wife's name was Elizabeth. They both loved God and tried to obey Him in everything they did. They were both getting older and they didn't have any children.

One day, when Zechariah was serving in the temple, an angel of the Lord appeared to him. When he saw the angel, he was startled and was very afraid. But the angel said to him, "Do not be afraid. Your prayers have been answered. Your wife, Elizabeth, will have a son and you are to name him John. You must dedicate him to the service of the Lord."

Zechariah asked the angel, "How can this happen? My wife and I are getting very old."

The angel said, "My name is Gabriel and I stand in the presence of God. He has sent me to give you this good news and you don't believe me?!? As a punishment, you will be unable to talk until the day your son is born."

The people outside the temple were waiting for Zechariah and wondering why it took him so long to come out. When he finally appeared, he couldn't speak to them. They realized he must have seen a vision because he kept making signs to them.

When he went home, his wife became pregnant. She knew right away that God had done this wonderful thing for her. She gave birth to a son. Her friends and relatives were very happy for her. All this time, Zechariah still was unable to talk.

Eight days after the baby was born, Elizabeth's family wanted to name the baby after Zechariah. Elizabeth said, "No, he is to be called John." Her family didn't want her to name the baby John because no one else in their family was named John.

They asked Zechariah what he wanted to name his child and he wrote down the words, "His name is John." Immediately, his mouth was opened and he began to speak, praising God.

Zechariah had learned a valuable lesson. We should never doubt anything that God tells us.

Lesson:
1. Read the story to your child.
2. Ask your child to imagine what it would be like not to talk for almost a full year.
3. Discuss how God wants us to believe Him – and we shouldn't doubt what He says to us in His Word.
4. See how long your child can go without talking. During this time, let your child use sign language, act out words, or any use other method they can think of to communicate – but no words. Time them.
5. Have a contest between yourself and your child to see who can go the longest without talking.

Lesson Ninety-Four – Praise Altar

Materials: Wagon or Bucket
                Picture of the Ark of the Covenant (see companion download)

Preparation: Print the Ark of the Covenant from the companion download.

Story:

Joshua was the leader of God's people when God was preparing to lead them into the land that He had promised to them. Joshua was a good man who loved God.

God told Joshua that He was getting ready to let all the people in the world know that He was with them. He told the priests who carry God's special Ark of the Covenant to go stand in the Jordan River. (Show your child the picture of the Ark of the Covenant from the companion download.) He said that as soon as they stepped into the river, the water would stop flowing and would pile up in a heap.

So God's people walked toward the Jordan River. It must have been a scary time because the Jordan River was very high this time of year. Imagine stepping into a river that is flooded! But the people believed God and obeyed his directions.

The priests walked out into the middle of the river and God stopped the river from flowing. All of God's people crossed the river and they walked through on dry ground!

Once everyone had crossed the river, God told Joshua to have twelve men go back into the riverbed and pick up a large stone. They were to use these stones to build a memorial to remember what God had done for them. The men did as the Lord had commanded.

All this time, the priests were still standing in the middle of the Jordan River holding the Ark of the Covenant. Once all the people were on the other side of the river, the Lord told the priests to come up out of the Jordan.

The priests obeyed. No sooner had they set their feet on dry ground than the waters of the Jordan started flowing again. God had helped His people to cross the river in an amazing way. The people praised God for taking such good care of them.

Lesson:
1. Read the story to your child.
2. Go for a walk with your child and collect fist-sized stones. Gather them in the wagon or bucket.
3. When you return home, explain to your child how Joshua made an altar to praise and worship God.
4. Take turns picking up stones and thanking God for a blessing (i.e., family, house, Jesus, friends, church, etc.)
5. As you say the praise, place the stone on the ground so that they form a pile.
6. Sing "God is so Good" with your child.

God is So Good
God is so good, God is so good,
God is so good, He's so good to me.

God cares for me, God cares for me,
God cares for me, He's so good to me.

God loves me so, God loves me so,
God loves me so, He's so good to me.

God answers prayer, God answers prayer,
God answers prayer, He's so good to me.

Lesson Ninety-Five – Shimei

Materials: Can of Spray Cheese or Whipped Cream
                Plastic Table Cloth (optional)

Preparation: Cover your table with the plastic table cloth for easier clean-up.

Story:

When David was king, he was traveling with his men. One day, they met a man named Shimei. He was from King Saul's family. Do you remember King Saul? He was the king before David.

Shimei was angry that David was the king. When he saw David, he started yelling awful things at him. He called him names. He even threw stones and dirt at David.

One of David's men couldn't stand it any longer. He asked David if he could hurt Shimei for all the things he was saying.

David had another plan. He calmly told the man to ignore Shimei. He told his men to continue walking and to ignore the insults that Shimei was saying. They were not to listen to the mean words. He encouraged his men and told them that God would take care of them.

It hurts when someone calls us a mean name. David felt that pain, too. Instead of hurting back, he chose to let God take care of the problem. Sure enough, Shimei came to David later and begged for forgiveness for saying such awful things. God took care of everything. When someone calls us names or is mean to us we should try to do what David did. We should ignore them and let God take care of the situation.

Lesson:
1. Read the story to your child.
2. Let your child squeeze the contents from the can onto the table.
3. Now have your child try to put the contents back into the can.
4. Discuss how easy it was to get the contents out of the can – but it's impossible to get it back into the can.
5. Discuss how mean words are like the cheese or the whipped cream. Once we say them, we can't take them back.

You Can Do All God Wants You To Do
God Wants You to Go To Church

Lesson Ninety-Six – Jesus at the Temple

Materials: Church Window (see companion download)
Contact Paper
Several Colors of Tissue Paper
Scissors
Glue

Preparation:
1. Print the church window from the companion download.
2. Using the printed church window as a template, cut out a piece of contact paper into the shape of a church window.

Story:

      When Jesus was a boy, he would travel with his family to Jerusalem for the Feast of Passover. They would make this trip every year.

      One time, when they made this trip, Jesus' family started back home. They thought Jesus was with them, but they had accidentally left him in Jerusalem. They were traveling with a large group of people, so it would have been easy for them to think that Jesus was with the rest of the children.

      They traveled for a day and then they noticed that Jesus wasn't with them. They turned back around and went to Jerusalem to search for their son. They searched for three days.

      Finally, they found him at the temple talking to the teachers. He was asking them questions and listening to their lessons. The teachers were amazed at how well Jesus could understand their teachings.

      When Jesus' parents saw him, they were upset at first. His mother said, "Son, why have you treated us poorly like this? We have been so worried about you!"

      Jesus said, "Why were you searching for me? Didn't you know that I'd be in my Father's house?"

      Jesus thought it was only natural that he would be at church learning about God. He wasn't trying to scare his parents or make them worry. He just knew that it was important for Him to spend time at church learning about God.

      God also wants us to spend time at church learning about Him.

Lesson:
1. Read the story to your child.
2. Discuss with your child how important it is for us to spend time in church learning about God.
3. Have your child rip small pieces off of several colors of their tissue paper.
4. Give your child the "church window."

5. Help them to tear the backing off of their church window and place it on the table sticky side up.
6. Let your child put their tissue paper pieces onto the contact paper to make a stained glass window.
7. When they're finished, you might want to tape them up to a real window. They will look their best when the light is shining through them.

Lesson Ninety-Seven – The Widow's Mite

Materials: A Handful of Pennies
                A Quarter
                A Small Jar

Preparation: None

Story:

One day, while Jesus was at the temple, he noticed some rich people. They were giving big gifts to God. They were pleased with themselves.

Then Jesus noticed a poor woman enter the temple. She only had two small copper coins left to her name. Jesus saw her walk forward and give them both to God.

The woman's gift was so much smaller than the rich people's gift had been; but, Jesus said that she gave the bigger gift. The rich people had so much money and they gave God just a small portion of everything they owned. The poor woman had almost no money and she gave God everything that she had.

God loves it when we give generously to him as did the poor woman.

Lesson:
1. Read the story to your child.
2. Give your child two pennies.
3. Give yourself ten pennies.
4. Pass the jar around and tell your child to put in two pennies. Then you put in two pennies. Show them that you have several pennies left over.
5. Discuss with your child how in the story one person gave everything they had while most of the people had plenty of money left over. Explain that God always rewards those who sacrifice for Him, while those who are greedy may have to depend on what they can get for themselves.
6. Give your child the quarter as a reward for giving everything that they had.

Lesson Ninety-Eight – One Body with Many Parts

Materials: Ballpoint Pen
                Piece of scrap paper

Preparation: Take the spring out of the pen and put it somewhere that you can find it easily.

Story:

      Did you know that God has given all of us different gifts and abilities? Some people play the piano well, some people sing beautifully, some people are strong, some are good teachers, some can paint, some share nicely, etc. We are all good at different things.

      God did that on purpose. He wants us to share our abilities with others. If God has made you good at coloring, He wants you to help other people color. If He has made you good at picking up toys, He wants you to help other people to pick up their toys.

      This is one reason we should go to church and help out while we're there. If everyone who loves God goes to church and uses their gifts there, then we can all help each other to be the best that we can be. We will also be able to tell more people about Jesus if we work together.

      Some people might think that their gift is too small to help anyone else. God says that everyone is needed to help out. If we all make up one body, you can think about it like this. It would be like the foot saying that because they aren't a hand, they don't need to help out. Or an ear saying that because they aren't an eye, they aren't important enough to help out. Isn't that silly?!? Are feet and ears important? Of course they are.

      Also, we should never think that someone else isn't important because their gift might be smaller than ours. A head should never say to a foot, "I don't need you." That wouldn't be true, would it? A head would never go anywhere if there weren't feet to take it somewhere.

      God wants us to value our gifts and He wants us to use them for the good of others.

Lesson:
1. Read the story to your child.
2. Hold up the pen. Ask your child what they think the most important part of the pen is.
3. Give them the pen and have them try to write with it. It won't work.
4. Hold up the spring. Talk about how it might see like a very small part, but that every part of the pen is important.
5. Put the spring back into the pen. Let your child write with it now.
6. Discuss how every person is important. Talk with your child about some of the gifts and abilities that you see in him. Discuss ways that your child might be able to help out at church. There are lots of things that preschool children can do to help out (i.e., sharing toys, emptying garbage, picking up trash, washing tables and chairs, etc.)

Lesson Ninety-Nine – Money Changers in the Temple

Materials: Various Coins
                     Crayons
                     Paper

Preparation: None

Story:

      Jesus went to church one day and saw men selling animals for a special celebration. Other men were changing Roman money into Jewish money so people could use their Jewish coins in church. Those sound like nice things to do, don't they? It sounds like these men wanted to help others by selling them what they needed.

      Jesus knew better. He knew what these men were really doing. Jesus knew that they wanted to make money for themselves. And making money isn't a bad thing – but these men were making money at church when they should have been learning about God.

      Jesus was very upset with these men.   He took ropes and tied them together to make a whip. Then, He made the animals and the people who were selling them leave. Jesus poured out the coins and turned over the tables of the money changers.

      Then Jesus told them that the church, God's house, was not a place for business. Jesus told them that when they came to church, they should come to pray. These men were not supposed to come to church thinking about making money. They were to come to church to learn about, think about, and talk to God.

Lesson:
1. Read the story to your child.
2. Help your child to make coin rubbings by placing the coins under the paper and rubbing the paper with the side of a crayon.
3. Talk with your child about how important it is to love God more than money.

Lesson One Hundred – Love One Another as I Have Loved You

Materials: Heart-Shaped Cookie Cutter
             Ingredients for Sugar Cookies (see companion
                Download for recipe)

Preparation:
1. Make the dough using the directions from the companion download.
2. Note: Dough for the cookies needs to be refrigerated for at least 2 hours before you can make the cookies!

Story:

If your mom or dad asks you to do something, do you think they are serious or are they just playing with you? Do you obey them the first time they ask you to do something? If they say something to you two or three times, what does that usually mean? It probably means that they are serious about what they are saying and it is important for you to listen and obey!

On the night before Jesus was going to die, Jesus told his disciples something. He didn't just say it once or twice. Jesus told them three times! Listen to what Jesus told His followers and see if you can tell me what He repeated three times. Jesus said, "I give you a new command. Love one another. You must love one another, just as I have loved you. If you love one another, everyone will know you are my disciples." What did Jesus say three times? Yes, He said, "love one another."

Jesus tells us that He wants us to love others the way He loves us. How is that? Well, He makes sure we have what we need. He shares with us. He cares for us.

Jesus also tells us why He wants us to love each other. When we love each other, the people around us can tell that we love God. And when people see that we love God, they will want to know and love Him, too!

Lesson:
1. Make the dough with your child if you haven't already done so.
2. Read the story to your child.
3. Make the heart-shaped cookies with your child and share them with someone who wasn't at church on Sunday.

Lesson One Hundred and One – Joash Cleans Up

Materials: Blocks
                    Kleenex

Preparation: None

Story:

Once, long ago, there was a king named Joash. He was only seven years old when he became king! They put a shiny gold crown on his head.

Joash lived with his aunt and uncle. They took care of him and he loved them very much. His uncle was a preacher who loved God. Joash's uncle told him many things about how much God loved him and cared for him. Joash loved God, too.

One day when Joash grew up, he saw how God's church was dirty and things inside were broken. He asked the preachers to collect money and repair the church.

After some time, Joash noticed the church still looked bad. He called the preachers into the palace and asked them why they had not worked on the church.

One of the preachers found a box and drilled a hole in the top. He put it in the church. He asked people to drop coins into the box to help fix God's church. Lots of people gave money to help clean up the church.

When the box was full, they gave the money to King Joash. When Joash got the money, he gave it to some men who hammered, sawed, and painted until the church looked beautiful. God was pleased that Joash and His people had repaired the church. Now it was a beautiful place to sing songs and worship God.

Lesson:
1. Read the story to your child.
2. Help your child to build a church with the blocks. Praise them for their excellent work.
3. Give your child a Kleenex to use as a feather duster to clean up the "church" they have built.
4. Sing fun songs as you work together.

Lesson One Hundred and Two – Don't Cheat God

Materials: Small Box
                   Sequins
                   Glitter
                   Glue

Preparation: None

Story:

Malachi was a man who loved God. He was also a prophet just as Elijah and Samuel had been. One day, Malachi had a special message to give to the people. The people had begun to doubt that God loved them. They thought that He had forgotten about them or didn't care about them anymore. God reminded them that He loves them. God also told the people that they had been cheating and robbing Him.

The people were shocked. They asked, "How have we cheated God?"

Malachi told them that they had forgotten to give God an offering or a tithe of the money they had received. A tithe is giving God a tenth of the money that you have earned. It is our way of thanking God for giving us the things we need and showing Him that He is first in our lives – not money. It also helps us to remember that everything we have belongs to God – and He lets us keep 90% of it – but He expects us to give 10% back to Him!

The people who respected God began to give as God commanded. They also told other people about God. Malachi 3:17 says that those who do this are a treasured possession to God. We'll be like sparkly diamonds – bright and beautiful to God.

Lesson:
1. Read the story to your child.
2. Discuss with your child how part of the reason we go to church is to give to God. We give our time and our money.
3. Talk about how your child is one of God's treasured possessions.
4. Make a treasure box with your child. Let them decorate their box with sequins and glitter.
5. NOTE: This will be messy! Keep a trashcan nearby to dump excess glitter into. Also, you may want to cover the working surface with newspaper for easier clean-up.

You Can Do All God Wants You To Do
God Wants You to Obey Your Parents

Lesson One Hundred and Three – Time Out

Materials: Blanket

Preparation: None

Story:

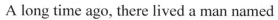

     A long time ago, there lived a man named Jonah. He loved God very much. He was also a man who gave people messages from God. One day, God told Jonah to go far away to the town of Nineveh and give the people a message. God wanted Jonah to warn them to turn from their wicked ways or He would destroy them.

     Jonah didn't like the people in Nineveh, so he decided to go the opposite direction. Jonah got on a ship and sailed far away. He was trying to hide from God. Jonah was so tired that he fell asleep on the boat.

     God knew where Jonah was. God made a huge storm come. It made the little boat toss wildly in the water. Everyone was very scared. They woke Jonah up.

     Jonah told them that it was his fault the storm had come. He told them he had disobeyed God and that God had sent the storm to stop him from running away. Jonah told them the only way to stop the storm was to throw him overboard into the sea.

     The people were shocked. They thought that Jonah would die if they threw him into the water. The storm got worse and worse, so finally they threw him into the water.

     Suddenly, the water was calm. The storm was gone. The people knew for sure that Jonah's God was the One True God. They worshipped God and told Him they were sorry for throwing Jonah into the water.

     God didn't want Jonah to die in the water; so, He sent a huge fish to swallow Jonah. While Jonah was in the fish, he had a lot of time to think about what he had done. Jonah told God he was sorry for not obeying His instructions.

     After three days, the fish spit Jonah out on land. He was close to the town of Nineveh, where God had wanted him to go in the first place.

     Jonah told the people God's message. The people were sorry about how they had disobeyed God. They asked God to forgive them.

     God did forgive them. Instead of punishing them as they deserved, God forgave them and told them how much He loved them.

     No matter how hard Jonah tried to get away from God, he ended up doing exactly what God wanted him to do. Wouldn't it have been easier if Jonah had obeyed God in the first place and had taken a boat to Nineveh instead of God having to swim him there in a fish?!?

Lesson:
1. Read the story to your child.
2. Discuss with your child how Jonah was being punished because he had disobeyed God. Talk about how God was punishing Jonah to try to teach him to obey. Tell you child that sometimes you have to punish them to teach them how to obey.
3. Have your child lie on the floor and cover them up with a blanket (including their head).
4. Have your child try to imagine that they are Jonah in the belly of the great fish. Ask them if it's dark… if it's quiet… if it's lonely.
5. After a few minutes, let your child get up and go do whatever they would like to in the house.
6. Ask your child which they liked doing better: being in the fish or doing whatever they wanted to do. Ask them to explain why?

Lesson One Hundred and Four – The Talking Donkey

Materials: Homemade Cookies

Preparation: Make one batch of cookies without sugar and one batch with sugar.

Story:

While Moses was the leader of God's people, they wandered in the desert for many years. God protected His people and they had more and more children. The kings of the lands they walked through didn't like God's people. They didn't want God's people to eat all their food. One of these kings was named Balak.

Balak wanted to have bad things happen to God's people so they couldn't want through his land. He heard of a man named Balaam who could wish bad things on people and these things would come true. King Balak asked Balaam to come to him and he would pay him lots of money.

Balaam spoke to God to find out what He would want him to do. God told him not to go to King Balak. He told him not to wish bad things on God's people. Balaam obeyed the Lord and didn't go to the king.

Not too much longer, King Balak sent more men to ask Balaam to come to him. He said he would pay him even more money to wish bad things on God's people. Balaam said he would have to speak to God to find out what He wanted him to do.

God gave Balaam permission to go to the king; but, He told him to only do what God would tell him to do.

Balaam got up in the morning, got on his donkey, and went with King Balak's men. But Balaam wasn't going for the right reason. He had started thinking too much about the money he would get and not enough about God. This made God angry. An angel of the Lord stood in the road to block Balaam.

When the donkey saw the angel of the Lord standing in the road with a sword in his hand, she turned off the road and walked into a field. Balaam couldn't see the angel; so, he beat the donkey to get her back on the road.

The angel stepped in front of the donkey again and this time she pressed close to a wall, crushing Balaam's foot against it. So Balaam beat her again.

Then the angel stood in a narrow space where there wasn't room to turn to the right or the left. When the donkey saw the angel, she lay down under Balaam. He was so angry that he beat her with her staff. God opened the donkey's mouth and the donkey said, "What have I done to you to make you beat me these three times?"

Balaam said, "You have made a fool of me! If I had a sword in my hand, I would kill you right now."

The donkey said, "You know me very well. Have I ever acted like this before?"

Then God opened Balaam's eyes and he saw the angel of the Lord standing in the road with his sword drawn. So he bowed low and fell face down. Balaam realized the donkey had saved his life. He asked the angel if he should turn back.

The angel told him he could keep going with the men, but he reminded him that he needed to obey God and only say what God wanted him to say. Balaam agreed – and this time he stopped thinking about King Balak's money and thought only of obeying God.

Lesson:

1. Read the story to your child.
2. Discuss with your child how Balaam had to learn a lesson about obeying because he tried to do something that God told him not to do.
3. Let your child taste a cookie without sugar (they will probably want to spit out their bite.)
4. Talk about how people sometimes look like they're doing the right thing on the outside; but, inside they're doing things for the wrong reason. Discuss how Balaam looked like he was obeying God; but, he wasn't necessarily doing what God wanted him to do.
5. Let your child enjoy a cookie with sugar.

Lesson One Hundred and Five – The Tower of Babel

Materials: Bag of Marshmallows
                Frosting or Peanut Butter
                Plastic Knife or Cheese Spreader

Preparation: None

Story:

After Noah had gotten out of the ark, God had given the command to spread out and fill up the whole earth. Noah's sons had many children, grandchildren and great-grandchildren. As more and more people were born, they began to ignore God's command to spread out. Many of the people settled in the same place and built a city.

After some time had passed, a group of men decided they would build a tower that would reach the heavens. They wanted to make a name for themselves and they wanted to be sure that God wouldn't spread them out over the whole earth.

God watched the men building their tower and He was very sad. He saw that the people weren't obeying Him. He saw how they were plotting together to do naughty things. So God decided to make all of these bad men speak different languages. That way, they wouldn't be able to understand each other anymore.

So God came down and caused the men to speak different languages. Then He scattered the people all over the earth, which caused them to stop building the city. From then on, they called the city Babel, which means "a confused mixture of sounds and voices."

When the people disobeyed God, He had to force them to do things His way. When children disobey, their parents have to punish them and force them to do things their way.

Next time your parents ask you to do something, be sure to obey right away. Don't be like the people at Babel who had to be punished to get them to do the right thing.

Lesson:
1. Read the story to your child.
2. Discuss how important it is to obey. Talk about punishment and why it is necessary – to train your child to make the right choices in the future.
3. Create a marshmallow tower out of the marshmallows. Use the frosting or peanut butter to "glue" the marshmallows together.

Lesson One Hundred and Six – Nehemiah

Materials: Boxes (big or small, your choice) – or blocks if you can't gather enough
                 boxes

Preparation: None

Story:

        Nehemiah was a man who helped the king. He was a cupbearer. His job was to taste the king's drink to make sure that no one had poisoned it. The king trusted him. The king liked Nehemiah and cared for him.
        One day, Nehemiah's brother told him some sad news. He discovered that the walls of his hometown, Jerusalem, were broken and had not been repaired. This troubled Nehemiah. He cried and prayed for several days. He had such a love for his beautiful city; he couldn't bear to see it in ruins.
        The next day, Nehemiah served the king his drink. The king immediately noticed that Nehemiah was upset. He asked him what was wrong.
        Nehemiah quickly prayed and then told the king and queen of his sadness. Then he boldly asked the king if he could go rebuild the city wall. After some talk, the king agreed.
        Nehemiah set out quickly. But he was careful about the things he did. In fact, when he got to Jerusalem, he kept his plans a secret.
        First, he went at night to look at the broken down wall. He rode a horse around the city and inspected it.
        Then, he talked to the people. He shared how God had answered his prayers and how the king let him come to help. Everyone was excited. They wanted to start rebuilding the wall right away.
        However, some people didn't like this plan. They asked lots of questions.
        What was Nehemiah's answer? He said, "We are God's servants. We will start rebuilding." He knew that God was helping them rebuild the wall. He wasn't going to let someone discourage them or stop the building.
        Nehemiah trusted God. He knew that God had answered his prayers. He had each person build the wall next to their home in the city. That was a good idea because everyone wanted to do their best job on the part that was by their home. They would work hard to make it safe and secure from their enemies.
        Several times, Nehemiah's enemies tried to stop the building. But each time, Nehemiah prayed to God for strength and courage.
        Guess what happened. They set a record! They finished the wall in 52 days!
        Even the enemies realized that only God could have done this because it was such a great, big wall.
        When the people completed the wall, Nehemiah helped them to worship God. They took time to read the Bible and obey God. It was a special time.
        Nehemiah knew that God answers prayers in three ways – yes, wait, and no. It is like a traffic light. The red light tells us to stop so we will not be hurt. God sometimes says "no" because it would not be a good thing for us.

A yellow light tells a driver to slow down and be cautious. God sometimes says "wait" or "slow down" and we have to wait for the prayer to be answered.

A green light is a signal for the driver to go ahead. God gives us green lights by answering our prayers with a "yes."

Nehemiah listened to God and did what He said. We must also listen to God and obey Him.

Lesson:
1. Read the story to your child.
2. Discuss with your child how Nehemiah obeyed God. Talk to them how learning to obey their parents is training for learning to obey God when they are older.
3. Use boxes to build a wall. While you are building, share with your child how a wall around a city would protect it from their enemies.

You Can Do All God Wants You To Do
God Wants You to Learn to Share Your Things with Others

Lesson One Hundred and Seven – Jesus Does a Miracle

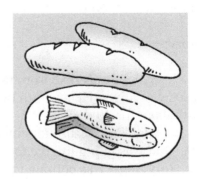

Materials: A Sandwich

Preparation: None

Story:

    Jesus was traveling and many people had come to hear Him talk about God. It was a special time to listen and hear how much God loved people and cared for everyone.

    When Jesus saw the crowd, He knew that they were far from their homes and that they were hungry because it was supper time. There were many, many people in the crowd. One of Jesus' disciples told Him that He needed to send the people away so they could find food.

    Jesus replied, "You give them something to eat."

    Another of Jesus' friends told Him that a little boy had brought five loaves of bread and two fish. Jesus asked His friends to bring Him the lunch.

    Jesus knew what He was going to do. He told His friends to tell the people to sit down. They did. All the people sat in groups. When they counted them, there were about 5,000 men – that's more people than in most large churches!

    Next, Jesus prayed, thanking God for the food. Then He broke the bread and the fish into pieces and He had His disciples pass some out to everyone. Every person ate as much as he wanted. They all ate until they were full.

    After they finished eating, Jesus had His disciples pick up the leftover pieces. The lunch had fed thousands of people and it took twelve baskets to hold all the leftovers! The people were amazed at the miracle that Jesus had done.

    One boy did the right thing and shared his lunch. God took that lunch and used it to feed lots and lots of people.

Lesson:
1. Read the story to your child.
2. Talk about how the boy shared his food and Jesus did a miracle with it to feed all of the people. Discuss how even if we think we're doing something small, God can take that action and make something big out of it.
3. Give your child their sandwich and encourage them to share half of it with someone else.

Lesson One Hundred and Eight – Jesus Goes to Heaven

Materials: None

Preparation: None

Story:

       After Jesus rose from the dead, His disciples and many other people saw Him. Jesus was alive. He ate with them. He talked to them about God and heaven. He was with them for 40 days.

       One day, Jesus ate with them. He told them not to leave but to wait for a big gift that God was going to give to them. It was a gift Jesus had told them about. Jesus said the Holy Spirit was coming to help them.

       Jesus said that His disciples would be strong when the Holy Spirit came to them. His helpers were to tell all the people in the whole world about Jesus.

       After Jesus said this, He rose into the sky and a cloud hid Him from his disciples.

Lesson:
1. Read the story to your child.
2. Discuss with your child how important it is to share the Good News about Jesus with others (how He was born on earth, died, and rose again – and now He sits at the right hand of the Father and intercedes for us.)
3. Play the "Pass It On" game with your child (family.) Say "Jesus loves you. Pass it on."

Lesson One Hundred and Nine – The Best Gift

Materials: None

Preparation: None

Story:

      Peter and John went to church one day. A man was there who could not walk. He asked Peter and John for money.

      Peter said, "Look at us!" The man looked at them.

      Peter said, "I do not have money, but I will give you what I do have. In the name of Jesus, walk."

      Peter took his hand to help the man get up. The man jumped up and walked. He walked and jumped and said thank you to God. Many men saw him walking and knew what God had done.

      The man held on to Peter and John and many men came to see what God had done. They were amazed!

      Peter asked the men why they were amazed. Peter said he didn't heal the man – God did it. Then Peter told them about Jesus. Peter told the men that God had sent His son to save them – and they had killed Him. Peter said he and John had seen Jesus alive – Jesus had risen from the dead.

      Peter said that this man loved Jesus and that is why he could now walk.

Lesson:
1. Read the story to your child.
2. Discuss with your child how the man wanted money and how Peter healed him instead of giving him money. Talk about how Peter was sharing the blessings that God had given to him with the lame man.
3. Ask your child how many different ways he can walk.
4. Have your child demonstrate hopping on one foot, walking backwards, walking like a duck, crawling like an alligator, doing the crabwalk, jumping high and running fast.
5. Ask your child if he thinks the man was happy when he was able to walk again and didn't just have to sit without moving his legs all day long.

Lesson One Hundred and Ten – Sharing All You Have

Materials: Muffin Mix (and necessary ingredients to bake)
                  Small Loaf Pan or Muffin Pan

Preparation: None

Story:

     Elijah was a man who loved God. Once, during this life, there was a terrible famine. There hadn't been any rain for a long time and it was hard to find food. God told Elijah to go to a certain city and find a woman who would provide him with food.

     Elijah obeyed God. He went to the city and found a woman whose husband had died. She was gathering sticks. Elijah asked her if she would please get him a drink of water. As she was going to get it, he also asked her for a piece of bread.

     "I'm sorry, I don't have any bread, "she said. "All I have is a handful of flour and a little bit of oil in a jug. I am gathering sticks to make a fire. I plan to make a small meal for me and my son. It won't be much food, though. So, soon after we eat it we will starve to death."

     Elijah told the woman not to be afraid. He told her to make some bread for him first and then to go back home and make food for herself and her son. "God says your flour and oil won't be used up until He sends rain again."

     The woman went away and did as Elijah had told her. Every day there was enough food for Elijah and for the woman and her son. The flour and oil never ran out and she and her son didn't starve to death. Because she was willing to share, she saved the lives of herself and her son.

Lesson:
1. Read the story to your child.
2. Discuss with your child how the widow shared what she had with Elijah, even though she didn't think she'd have enough food for her son. Talk about how God blessed her because she was unselfish.
3. Bake a small loaf of bread (or muffins) with your child using the muffin mix. After the bread has cooled, share the bread with each other.

Lesson One Hundred and Eleven – Salt and Light

Materials: Salty Snacks (i.e., Nuts, Popcorn, Chips, etc.)
Unsalty Snacks (i.e., Carmel Corn, Unsalted Popcorn, Graham Crackers)
Water or Juice

Preparation: None

Story:

     Jesus talked to many, many people about God. He taught them lots of things and shared how they should live. He liked to use symbols to help the people understand. One time, Jesus talked about salt and light.

     Jesus told the people that they should be like salt. People use salt to make things taste good. People also use salt to preserve food. That means the salt makes the food stay good instead of becoming rotten.

     Jesus told the people that they should be like the salt – helping others and being a person that others like to be around. We should also help others know Jesus so that they can go to Heaven and be with God forever.

     Jesus also told the people that they needed to be like a light. He explained that a person shouldn't hide his light under a basket or a bowl. No! He should let it shine for all to see. Jesus was telling His friends that they should not be ashamed of Jesus and hide Him. They should let others know how much they loved Him and how He has changed their lives.

     Jesus told the people that if they shine their lights, people will see them and thank God in Heaven for all the good things that the people have done.

     Jesus wants us to share our time and our talents with people by helping them. He also wants us to share the Good News about Jesus with people so they can have a chance to go to Heaven someday.

Lesson:
1. Read the story to your child.
2. Have a fun taste test. Let your child try the unsalted things first. Then let them try the salted things. (They would probably like some juice or water to wash down the snacks.)
3. Talk about the difference. Ask them how we can be like the salty things.

Lesson One Hundred and Twelve – Sheep and Goats

Materials: A Snack
                Juice or Water
                One of their Daddy's shirts
                Band-Aid

Preparation: None

Story:

      Jesus wanted to help His friends know what it will be like when He comes back. He told another story to help us understand what will happen and how to be ready.

      Jesus' story is about sheep and goats. When a shepherd gathers his sheep, he doesn't want any goats in the flock. He has to separate them. He puts the sheep on one side and the goats on the other side.

      Jesus explained that when He comes back, He will gather all the people of the world together. He will separate those who believe in Him (on His right) from those who do not believe in Him (on His left.)

      On that day, Jesus will say, "I knew that you loved Me. When I was hungry you gave Me food. When I was thirsty you gave Me something to drink. When I didn't have any clothes you gave Me something to wear. When I was sick you cared for Me. When I was in prison you visited me."

      The believers will then answer, "When did we see You and do these things?"

      Jesus will answer, "When you helped someone in need, you were helping Me and showing ME that you believed in Me and wanted to do what I said. You will be in Heaven with Me!"

      Those who do not believe in Jesus will be on His left. He will say to them, "I knew that you didn't love Me. When I was hungry you didn't give Me food. When I was thirsty you didn't give Me something to drink. When I didn't have any clothes you didn't give Me something to wear. When I was sick you didn't care for Me. When I was in prison you didn't visit me."

      The people will say, "When did we see You and not do these things?"

      Jesus will respond, "When you refused to help anyone who was in need, you were refusing to help Me."

      Jesus says that if we love Him, we must show it by helping people when they need it. We need to share our time, our talents, and our money with others. That is how Jesus will know that we truly love Him.

Lesson:
1. Read the story to your child.
2. Act out the ways that we can show Jesus we love Him. Use these props/actions at the appropriate times:
     · Hungry = give them a snack   · Sick = have them put on a band-aid
     · Thirsty = give them juice or water   · Prison = say "hello" and give them a hug
     · Without clothes = let them try on one of Daddy's shirts